JUMPSTART!
POETRY

The *Jumpstart!* books contain 'quick-fire' ideas that could be used as warm-ups and starters as well as possibly extended into lessons. There are more than 100 provocative games and activities for Key Stage 1, 2 or 3 classrooms. Practical, easy-to-do and vastly entertaining, the 'jumpstarts' will appeal to busy teachers in any primary or Key Stage 3 classroom.

Also available in the series:

Jumpstart! Creativity
Games and Activities for Ages 7–14
078-0-415-43273-7
Steve Bowkett

Jumpstart! ICT
ICT Activities and Games for Ages 7–14
978-1-84312-465-8
John Taylor

Jumpstart! Literacy
Games and Activities for Ages 7–14
978-1-84312-102-2
Pie Corbett

Jumpstart! Numeracy
Maths Activities and Games for Ages 5–14
978-1-84312-264-7
John Taylor

Forthcoming:

Jumpstart! Storymaking
Games and Activities for Ages 7–12
978-0-415-46686-8
Pie Corbett

JUMPSTART!
POETRY

GAMES AND ACTIVITIES FOR AGES 7–12

Pie Corbett

Routledge
Taylor & Francis Group

LONDON AND NEW YORK

First published 2008
by Routledge
2 Park Square, Milton Park, Abingdon, Oxon, OX14 4RN

Simultaneously published in the USA and Canada
by Routledge
270 Madison Ave, New York, NY 10016

Routledge is an imprint of the Taylor & Francis Group, an informa business

British Library Cataloguing in Publication Data
A catalogue record for this book is available from the British Library.

Library of Congress Cataloging in Publication Data
Corbett, Pie.
Jumpstart! Poetry: games and activities for ages 7–12 / Pie Corbett.
  p. cm.
ISBN 978-0-415-46708-7 (pbk.)
1. Poetry–Study and teaching (Elementary) 2. Poetry–Authorship–Study
and teaching (Elementary) [1. Games.] I. Title.
LB1576.C7183 2008
372.64–dc22

                                                                    2008018505

ISBN 10: 0-415-46708-7 (pbk)
ISBN 13: 978-0-415-46708-7 (pbk)

Typeset in Palatino/Scala Sans by FiSH Books, Enfield
Printed and bound in Great Britain by Antony Rowe, Chippenham,
Wilts

Contents

Where there is no vision, the people perish.

Proverbs 29:18

For Melanie – inspiring teacher of writing and art

Acknowledgements

Many of these activities have been developed over the years with different classes and teachers – and I would like to give credit to all those teachers and children who have assisted in helping me to develop ideas, especially the poet Brian Moses. The reading games are obviously influenced by the work of Lunzer and Gardener's DARTS (Directed Activites Related to Texts). However, the games are also influenced by the Surrealists and Dadaists, who enjoyed playing poetry games, as well as more recent poetry activities mainly developed in America by writers such as William Burroughs, Brion Gysin and the school of poetics that appropriate, innovate or define procedures for creating new ways of looking at language – for instance, writers such as John Cage, Ted Berrigan, Ron Padgett and Jackson Mac Low.

Writing ideas are influenced by the educational writings of both Ted Hughes and Kenneth Koch. Two sides of the poetry coin that I have attempted to bring together. My own interest in poetry writing was kindled by the influence of the Liverpool Poets whose poems entered my imaginative world and made me believe and want to write my own poems.

Some of these ideas have appeared on the Everybody Writes website (http://www.everybodywrites.org.uk/), courtesy of the National Book Trust. The main ideas were explored in a series of conferences organized with the National Literacy Trust and the Basic Skills Agency. Many of the ideas formed part of the National Primary Strategy 'Talk for Writing' initiative, involving every primary school. I would also like to thank the children whose examples I have used, especially those from Chalford Primary. All examples and models are by myself, unless otherwise accredited.

Introduction

THE POET'S CHARM

By the slim pencil,
By the tender writing,
By the blank page,
Come to life.

By the point of the nib,
By the dark writing,
By the loping rhythm,
Come to life.

Katya, 7 yrs

Children write best about what they know, what matters and what amuses the mind. They should love writing and if they do not enjoy words then they will never become comfortable with writing. The aim of *Jumpstart! Poetry* is to build up a bank of ideas that can be drawn upon when teaching poetry but also at other times to provide a source for creative writing that children will relish.

Children's writing is influenced by their reading. Many children are familiar with the cheerful collections of poetry in the 'My Dad smells like a wet dog' vein of bums and bogies. Whilst this may capture interest, a creative classroom will need to plunge deeper, richer and broader to provide a powerful bank of language possibilities and poetic inclinations. Avid readers internalize a sense of what is elegantly constructed, playfully, powerfully and surprisingly written. Techniques may be encountered but, more importantly, a sense of what poems can do – poems can lie, imagine, pretend, comment, describe, question, command, defy, wonder, riddle, contrast, personify, even speak to tigers! Reading poetry aloud and performing poems are of key importance in helping children love poetry, as well as building themselves a repertoire to draw upon. The danger of a content heavy national curriculum is that we end up hopping from one thing to another like a shallow stream dimpling on its way. . .as we dip and weave through an overloaded curriculum.

At the heart of creative writing lies experience – real and imagined. Something worth writing about – a focus that intrigues, that demands language used in a special way. Years ago, I took some town children to a youth hostel. At night we went outside. They stood and stared at the Moon. It was a crisp, autumn night and the Moon was full and silvery white. Somehow, just saying 'we saw the Moon and it was big' would not do the experience justice. It demanded language to be used in a special way to communicate the enormity, the silvery light, the ghostly eye and the crisp pinch of darkness.

Recently, I was running a day-long workshop for able writers. We had been looking at some photographs of bees on the interactive whiteboard. They were taken close up so that the eyes bulged. A ten year old boy began his poem like this:

Cloudy petals lie, drowsy, sleeping.

Pollen rests, conscious
of its fragile beauty.

How is it that he, probably unconsciously, selected the words 'cloudy' and 'drowsy', creating an internal echo where the slow, soft vowel sounds pillow the sentence? And then he followed this with 'sleeping' where the 'ee' slows the line further? Not surprisingly, he reads. Perhaps his reading has helped him acquire a sensitive ear so that he can hear whether a line works or not. He can make judgements. Of course, if you haven't read beautiful writing then it is impossible to write beautifully or know when you have written powerfully.

And what are we to make of a 10-year-old boy who writes 'pollen rests, conscious of its fragile beauty'? Or who ends his poem with an extended metaphor:

Cloudy petals lie, drowsy, sleeping.

Pollen rests, conscious
of its fragile beauty.

Delicate wings dream dormant frozen
in the chilling wind.

Legs weak like the stroke
of a fine meandering brush.

Glaring eyes powerfully dart
in all directions staring,
wondering.

The bee
is a master of disguise,

hiding in the autumn brown
of a fragile leaf,

camouflaging himself
in the gold of the sleeping pollen,

secretly lying in the cover
of blossoming flowers.

It made me wonder how a boy like this will fare when presented with SATs or the new idea of testing when children are ready. Surely writing of this order suggests a sensitivity towards language, the ability to observe, feel and celebrate the essence of experience. It is a far stretch from being asked to write a police report about an accident that never happened!

So, this little book is about involving children as creative writers. It might be worth them keeping a writing journal and developing the habit of collecting words and noticing ideas, jotting down phrases and lines that might prove useful. Good ideas, snippets from the games and whole poems should be stored in their journal. They need to become 'word-searchers' as well as being 'observers' of the world. Writers are good at looking; they notice the details that suggest something deeper, the details that illuminate. They are also attuned to word choices that illuminate and surprise the reader. The results of quick writing games may be worth storing so that lines or images may be plundered when children are writing at length.

Providing interesting writing tasks is essential to motivating children. To strengthen children's imagination, you have to enter into a place close to their own sense of excitement. Whilst much of their writing can be based on using real experiences, they should also spend plenty of time playing with words and ideas. Many of the writing games in this book involve learning that language is the material for creating and can be moved around to fashion all sorts of new and fascinating combinations.

I wonder if many boys ignore writing because the tasks are lifeless and the writing leads nowhere. It stays trapped inside an exercise book with the teacher spitting from the margins. Perhaps too much writing that boys encounter is concerned with 'whole texts' rather than short-burst creative tasks. Boys are minimalists and poetic writing often suits their sense of fun and creativity. Modern technology has made it so easy to publish posters, booklets and anthologies – let alone creating blogs, web sites or multimedia texts with sound, video, images and writing. Publishing in various formats should be a regular part of the creative classroom – we create to communicate. Publishing is a potent force that focuses children on the need to write effectively.

This book is a collection of ideas gathered over 35 years of involvement in writing and teaching poetry. In the main, they are intended as quick-fire warm-ups to fire the brain into a creative mood for reading or writing. These sorts of linguistic gymnastics help establish an atmosphere and prepare the ground for in-depth reading, writing and performance. Of course, some may become extended into a whole session. Good writing does not always arrive fully formed – but the nuggets from these games can be stored away for future use. These activities are part of limbering up and may sometimes generate something which may be useful elsewhere. There are multi-sensory games to develop the imagination, practise techniques, generate creative thinking, to stimulate the writing of poems as well as reading games and workshops.

I do think that it would be very interesting to see what would happen to a child's writing if they had to write a quick-fire poetry idea every day for a year – say ten minutes writing daily. The golfer Gary Player said, 'The more I practise, the luckier I get.' Pianists practise scales, weight-lifters go to the gym. Surely, if children are to 'get lucky' and become good at writing they should be involved in the daily tussle with words. The creative writing workshop is about 'hands on' – the business of crafting language and ideas.

A good poetry idea should help the children feel excited about writing and enable them to think of what to write. A good idea is both an invitation as well as a catalyst. This may need some scaffolding – making lists, brainstorming ideas and plenty of 'having a go together' – to create a class example. Alongside this, it is worth bearing in mind the advice of the American poet Kenneth Koch when he said, about working with children, 'perhaps the most important thing to do, I found, is to be positive about everything'. It is sad that this simple idea is so rare in our world of tests, data and league tables where most writing is used to reveal a child's ignorance or at best is accomplished to determine a level of attainment.

The ideas should act as catalysts that generate thinking and language play. Other ideas should be allowed to creep in and gatecrash the party. Soon you will develop an eye for poems that suggest a writing idea or a line that lends itself to innovation or a game for playing with words. Add to this poetic storehouse – and keep sharing with other teachers.

A final note: For simplicity's sake, the poems I mention are found in the anthology, *The Works: Poems for Key Stage 2* (2006), published by Macmillan Children's Books, edited by myself. In this book, I specifically collected poems that I would want to use with children from 7 through to about 12 years old. Many are classic workshop poems – ideal as a stimulus to writing or with sufficient depth for sustaining reading.

CHAPTER 1

Ideas for developing a 'poetry climate' in schools and classrooms

Children love reading, writing and performing poetry. It is essential to our well-being because it focuses upon creativity. . . and creativity matters, especially for those with chaotic lives. It is worth remembering that the opposite of creation is destruction. It seems an obvious idea to work out which poets are going to become the main focus for teaching with a poet a term. This means that the children become familiar with a range of poets over time. For instance:

Year Group	Poets
Year 3	June Crebin
	James Carter
	Michael Rosen
Year 4	Charles Causley
	Alan Ahlberg
	Jan Dean
Year 5	Valerie Bloom
	Brian Moses
	Kit Wright
Year 6	Ted Hughes
	William Blake
	Judith Nichols

Year 7	Roger McGough
	Jackie Kay
	Carol Ann Duffy
Year 8	Brian Patten
	Matthew Sweeney
	Grace Nicols
Year 9	Philip Gross
	John Agard
	Helen Dunmore

RHYME OF THE WEEK

At key stage 1 children need to learn a bank of nursery, traditional and action rhymes. Many picture books rhyme (*Each Peach Pear Plum*) and there are a few 'key' poems such as 'The Owl and the Pussy Cat' that should be learned and performed. Poetry at key stage 1 should be a daily occurrence and this is achieved by establishing a 'poem of the week'. It is worth remembering that there is a strong link between success in reading and experience in rhyming. In many classes the idea of 'rhyme of the week' needs to be carried on into year 3.

POEM OF THE DAY

During key stage 2 and 3 establish a routine of 'poem of the day'. Draw up a simple rota with children's names. Each day it is somebody else's turn to perform a poem. This could be read aloud or learned. It might be a solo poem or friends can be involved. Once a week, the teacher reads a poem in order to model effective reading. This is a simple method of broadening children's repertoire and helping them to internalise patterns, rhythms and ideas.

If you have a climate of curiosity about poetry and enjoyment then you may find that children write poems and little fragments off their own bat; especially if you have provided a writing journal. Billy Collins wrote tellingly about the influence of reading poetry on his writing – how good poetry can act not only as a celebration but also as an invitation. In *The Trouble with Poetry* (Random House, 2005) he says that reading poetry makes him want to write poetry. He describes waiting in the darkness, holding a pencil and hoping for a flame to spark his writing.

That is what we have to try to kindle in the classroom – thousands of little flames, so that children actually want to write. If they do not enjoy writing then something is wrong. We need to find poems like little gifts that make the children want to write.

20 WAYS TO ESTABLISH A POETRY CLIMATE

1. Display poems around the classroom and school – in staff rooms, on the backs of doors, on notice boards.
2. As a school, decide to read 'a poem a day' – perhaps from one of the Macmillan *Read Me* books. Have 'poet of the week', or each term every class focuses on a different poet.
3. Include a poem in all assemblies.
4. Create a 'poet tree' that has different branches (for different types of poem and for poets, e.g. the haiku branch, the Charles Causley branch). On the leaves the children copy up lines, verses or poems.
5. 'Desert Island Poems' – read out your favourites and explain what it is you like about the poem.
6. Poem swap – find a poem for a friend and swap over.
7. Put poems on to cards – children take a poem card home. Favourites can be learned by heart or performed.
8. Tape a poetry programme – or get pupils to make a Power Point of poems transposed on to images or photos.
9. Start all staff meetings with a poem.
10. Each teacher sends a poem as a message to another teacher every Friday morning for a term!

3

11. Put a haiku on every newsletter.
12. Create and sell CDs or DVDs of children reading or performing their poems and stories and sell these.
13. Annual school anthology of children's poetry.
14. Use poems across the curriculum (*The Works 2 – Poems on every subject and for every occasion*, published by Macmillan Children's Books, 2002).
15. Use screen savers to show haiku.
16. Make pottery slabs with brief poems or lines printed on each slab.
17. Paint and display poetry banners and flags.
18. Use English teachers to make links with other subjects so that poems are written that accompany science or history, art or music, or dance.
19. Put on a poetry performance that involves poems, dances, music and drama.
20. Read, perform and celebrate poetry beyond the confines of the exam syllabus.
21. As a staff, brainstorm other ideas – have a poetry noticeboard in the staffroom.

CHAPTER 2
Poetry reading games and activities

DIGGING DEEPER

Poems are not like sums – they do not always easily add up. It seems to me more important for a child to enjoy a poem than to have an opinion about it. What we can say for sure is that when reading poetry, it is important to read it aloud. Poems are nearly always to be heard as well as read in the head. It is the combination of sound and meaning that has the full impact.

Here are some activities that will help children dig under the skin of a poem. Remember that the aim is for children to enjoy and take to heart a poem. Trying to spot powerful verbs may just make the whole activity rather meaningless. All reading of poetry should involve both performing and discussing. But there are many other ways into a poem. Reading, performing and discussing are important, but games where the children interact with the poem may also help them to become more intimate with the poem. Try playing with the poem. You are aiming for them to become attached to its rhythms and patterns, images and words. Choose the games that suit the poem:

- Put children into pairs to make a list about a poem of likes, dislikes, puzzles and patterns. Or, each pair makes a list of five questions they are curious about. Later on, list these as a class and see if other pairs can provide ideas or answers.

- Select the five most important words – if you had £1 and words cost 10p, which words would you buy?
- Jot down your initial ideas, memories, questions, thoughts, similar experiences and feelings, and share these in pairs.
- What was the most powerful picture?
- Annotate the poem – make statements or raise questions.
- Prepare a group reading of a poem. Think about how to use voices, varying the pace, expression and volume to suit the meaning. Make sure the words are clear – add in percussive backing where relevant.
- Compare readings by different groups – what suited the poem best and why?
- Cut a poem up by verses, lines or words to be re-sequenced, e.g. try reassembling the poem on the next page.

Cut-up version ready for children to reassemble into their own version	My original

A bright bus blunders
a cyclist sidles by.
are sending morse-code.
Black taxis scuttle
Dark streets yawn.
down back alleys.
Goodnight Stroud
   It's late –
Its hands fidget
like wet toads;
Parked cars huddle
   restless as rain.
that the stars
The belisha beacon blinks.
The clock tower glowers.
the night thinks
the streets wait –
towards dawn.
Trains idle up sidelines;
up the High Street.
	Goodnight Stroud
	
	The clock tower glowers.
	Its hands fidget
	towards dawn.
	
	Dark streets yawn.
	   It's late –
	the streets wait –
	   restless as rain.
	
	Trains idle up sidelines;
	a cyclist sidles by.
	
	Black taxis scuttle
	down back alleys.
	
	A bright bus blunders
	up the High Street.
	
	The belisha beacon blinks.
	
	Parked cars huddle
	like wet toads;
	the night thinks
	that the stars
	are sending morse-code.

- Explain the poem to a friend.
- Give children a poem without the title – what is it called ('Car Pets')? E.g.

The car squats
at the side of the road
iron-still –

all night it waits,
not budging a jot,
not twitching a muscle

but under the bonnet
lives a family of car pets.

Grateful for
the crumbs of crisps
scattered on the back seat

and cool water sipped
from the radiator,
they feel the wind's speed,
need the throaty roar
of the engine

as the wheels grab
the road.

- Use a colour to identify powerful words or surprising images.
- Use two colours – one for sound effects (alliteration, onomatopoeia, rhymes, hard/soft sounds) and another colour for pictures (similes, metaphors). Discuss choices.
- Omit key words and present a poem as a cloze procedure.
- Respond to the poem in another form, e.g. a letter, diary entry, message, newspaper article.
- Illustrate a poem and annotate with words and images.
- Interview the poet or poem in pairs.
- Let the poet talk aloud, 'I've just written a poem about. . .'.
- Interview the poet or 'Professor Poet' (world's poetry expert) and use the words, 'Tell me about. . .' to start the interview's questions. The interviewer should have a list

of things that can be asked, all starting with the words 'tell me about. . .'. Children work in pairs, one in the role of the poet (or poem) and the other about to interview them. Read a poem. The interviewers then ask questions and role-play an interview. Hear some in front of the class. Questions can be about the poem, but also any other aspect that the interviewer deems interesting. This game might be handy after several weeks of hearing different daily poems by a poet.

- Hot seat characters or creatures in a poem.
- Rewrite a poem that is written out in prose form: e.g.

EARLY WINTER DIARY POEM

(18th November 1999)

Six-thirty; winter dawn – scraping a thin skin of frost from the windscreen – numb fingers fumble – even the spray freezes. The breeze is bitter – it's so cold that stones crack – that wool freezes on the sheep's back. The birds are too still – even the sun turns its back on the day; but lazy wood-smoke idles over Minchin's roof.

EARLY WINTER DIARY POEM

(18th November 1999)

Six-thirty;
   winter dawn –

scraping a thin skin
   of frost
from the windscreen –
   numb fingers fumble –
even the spray freezes.
   The breeze is bitter –
it's so cold
   that stones crack –

9

> that wool freezes
> on the sheep's back.
>
> The birds are too still –
> even the sun
> turns its back
> on the day;
> but lazy wood-smoke
> idles
> over Minchin's roof.

- Read a poem aloud but change a word, several words, phrases or even a line. Can the children spot the alteration? This is a sort of 'aural' cloze procedure.
- Do the same as above but skip a line. Can the children spot where you omitted a line?
- Try the same approach but swap words over within the poem. Of course, the last three games could be presented in writing – but try them orally.
- Compare two or three short poems. Which is best and why? Make statements to support your poem.

> Midnight streetlights.
> Frost glistens;
> tiny stars
> make a universe
> on the pavement.

> Lightning cracks –
> shattering the night
> into glassy splinters
> of electric light –
> a whiplash of static.

> Snow muffles
> the streets;
> transforming bushes
> into brides.
> White confetti settles.

- Present a poem on the page but omit the ending of every line. Can the children work out what is missing? This is a form of cloze procedure that focuses attention on the ends of lines. You could just as well take out the beginning or middle section – again, another form of cloze procedure.

My original	Without end rhymes
LENT	**LENT**
This year I'm giving up time –	This year I'm giving up –
Time to keep my bedroom clean,	Time to keep my bedroom ,
Time to clear the kitchen table,	Time to clear the kitchen ,
Time to sweep the backyard,	Time to sweep the ,
Time to help when I am able.	Time to help when I am .
Time to do my homework,	Time to do my ,
Time to run down to the shops,	Time to run down to the ,
Time to carry heavy bags,	Time to carry heavy ,
Time to help Mum when she stops –	Time to help Mum when she –
And sits down for a cup of tea –	And sits down for a cup of –
Time to give others time,	Time to give others ,
And in the end, some time for me.	And in the end, some time for .

- Read the poem backwards.
- Provide a bank of musical clips. Which would suit the poem best as a background for reading?
- Provide a bank of images. Which would work best?
- Put the music, images and group reading together so that each group performs its own multimedia presentation.
- William Burroughs suggested cutting a poem down the middle and across the centre. Present it as four pieces and reassemble it to make a new combination – read the variants aloud. Try cutting off corners and swapping them over, or make other shapes, e.g. 'Eternity' by William Blake.

Original	Cut-up version
He who bends to himself a joy Does the winged life destroy; But he who kisses the joy as it flies Lives in eternity's sunrise.	But he who kisses to himself a joy Lives in eternity's life destroy; He who bends the joy as it flies Does the winged sunrise.

- Omit the fourth and sixth word in every line; or any other variant.
- Take two poems or nursery rhymes of about the same length (see left-hand column below). The game is to blend the two rhymes together. This could be done in many ways. For instance, you could use alternate lines from each rhyme. Try swapping words over between rhymes or alternating verses. Let groups experiment by creating different versions. Allow for readjustment to spelling and grammar. The idea is to take two rhymes and mix them up in order to create something new.

Original rhymes	Blended version with minor adjustment
Jack Sprat Had a cat, It had but one ear; It went to buy butter When butter was dear. * Jerry Hall, He is so small, A rat could eat him, Hat and all.	Jack Sprat He is so small, A rat could eat him, So he had a cat, Hat and all. It had but one ear. Poor Jerry Hall, Went to buy butter When butter was dear.

- Try gradually revealing a poem on the interactive whiteboard using a spotlight function. Keep pausing to tease the class. What is the poem about? Let them pile up the clues as more is revealed.
- Provide a poem in another language or old English or a made-up language (see below) and ask for a translation.

This will mean guessing. It helps if you can read it aloud (or use a recording of, say, an extract from 'Beowulf') so that the class can hear the words.

> A rigdum pordum duo coino.
> Col min ero giltee caro
> Bree darlit conzee shardik,
> Stim stam pammedarv
> Lara bradst sungstan,
> fregarv straquiv duo caldecit.

- Turn a poem into a cartoon with, say, six boxes. What are the key six main images or scenes? What captions should accompany them? This is good for story poems but also any sort.
- Write three statements and three questions about the poem – swap these over so that partners can write replies to their partner's questions.
- Individuals or groups mime the poem. Mime different poems. Read the poem aloud to the mime.
- Children mime a line from the poem. Who can guess which line is being mimed?
- Record three readings of the poem – each read in very different ways. Children discuss which is the best reading and why.
- Children are asked to work in groups to prepare a reading of a poem. Give each group a focus for their reading. After the performances discuss which was most powerful and why. Possible focuses might include: read this as a rap; vary soft and loud; vary speed; sing it; use body percussion; read angrily; read calmly; use shouts and whispers; use mime and voices. . .
- Children discuss the poem, using a series of prompts that they can select from. Prompts might include:
  - What do you notice in the poem?
  - What is it about?
  - What happens in the poem?

- How does the poet make an impact on the reader?
- Describe the main scene/image. What is going on?
- Talk about the ideas in the poem.
- What did the poem make you think about?
- What did the poem remind you of?
- Use a frame to write about the poem, e.g.:

What the poem is/seems to be about.
Why I have chosen it – likes, dislikes and puzzles.
What the poem means to me.
What the poem reminds me of/makes me think about.
The poem's pattern and the techniques and language used and their impact.
Final comment – most memorable aspect.

- Exploring feelings in a poem: choose a key image from a poem that made you feel something (happy? sad? bored?) and explore why: *'The Tyger' made me feel sad because...*
- Thoughts in the head: draw a cartoon or thought bubble for a character in a story poem. Hot seat the character or have them perform a monologue.
- Rumours and lies: make up some lies about the poem. In other words make a series of statements that certainly are untrue.
- The muddled haiku: take some haiku and cut them up line by line. This is easiest done on the computer. Now jumble up the lines, perhaps placing them in alphabetical order. Photocopy the result. The children have to sort the lines out and create new haiku. (This is easiest if you remove the punctuation.) The phrases provided here are shown in their original haiku form in the game that follows. Incidentally, in line with most western writers of haiku I do not use 5/7/5 syllables but aim for a short poem that can be spoken in one breath.

a cicada rings
a contented Buddha
a hawk in sultry heat
a lazy lizard agrees
a road of stars
a sky anchor
a sudden gust
a wasp sting
a white moon
bees busy
but the pool is cool
butterflies dizzy past
cherry blossoms
contemplates the sunflower
crazy ants
even the pillows sweat
fidgeting, restlessly
flies stalk the cup's rim
frost glistens
fuss by the pool
in slim pastel-blue
in the midnight fountain
in the valley hangs
melt on your cheek
mercury in my hand
midnight streetlights
moonlight crumples
on a mission to nowhere
pencil dragonflies
rises on your arm
shivering
the hills shimmer
the room is too stuffy
the tabby cat
trying to sleep
washing hands

- Desert island haiku: in this game provide a series of, say, ten haiku. The children work in pairs to produce an order, ranking the poems from 1 to 10 in order of their preference. Then put the children into fours and see if they can agree on the top five. Then move to groups of eight and see if they can agree on a top three. Remember that this is to encourage the children to justify their choices to get them reading and re-reading.

Midnight streetlights; frost glistens – a road of stars.	In the valley hangs a hawk in sultry heat; a sky anchor.	The tabby cat contemplates the sunflower; a contented Buddha.
Crazy ants fuss by the pool on a mission to nowhere.	Bees busy; butterflies dizzy past. A lazy lizard agrees.	Pencil dragonflies in slim pastel-blue; shivering.
A wasp sting – a white moon rises on your arm.	Flies stalk the cup's rim. Washing hands – fidgeting, restlessly.	Trying to sleep – the room is too stuffy. Even the pillows sweat.
A sudden gust – cherry blossoms melt on your cheek.	The hills shimmer but the pool is cool. A cicada rings.	In the midnight fountain moonlight crumples mercury in my hand.

- Illustrated haiku: give out some haiku – the children select their favourite and then illustrate within a time limit. The game is to see if the others can guess which haiku has been illustrated.
- Imitation reading game: read a short poem to the class. The game is for the children to listen carefully and then, as soon as you have finished, they should write down as much as they can remember, filling in gaps if they need. In pairs, they can compare results and then listen to the original again. This develops memory but is also

interesting because different people remember different sections – or everyone remembers the same piece. Why? Discuss the memorable aspects – was it rhythm, the image, the word combination, its impact? An alternative or addition is to read the poem and the children make a free-flowing sketch or visual mind map to represent the words. These are interesting if you can get examples on to the interactive whiteboard for the class to discuss.

• Poetry innovations: select a line or phrase and imitate. Use this as a pattern for the children to innovate. For instance, a phrase from the opening of Blake's 'The Tyger' could be used:

> In the forests of the night
> In the tunnels of the dark
> In the ocean of the sky
> In the silence of the stone
> In the chatter of the trees
> In the mazes of the ground

Innovations can be based on a single phrase or line – all the way through to imitating a whole poem, such as 'The Magic Box'.

DESIGNING A POETRY UNIT

Every poetry unit should involve children reading, writing and performing poems. Many teachers like to use the national framework as a guide but new enthusiasms should not be ignored.

Year 5/6 unit
• Read, annotate and discuss – 'The Highwayman' by Alfred Noyes.
• Prepare choral class performance for assembly.
• Draw cartoon version.
• Interview main characters in role as journalists.

- Write newspaper accounts.
- Read, annotate and discuss – 'The Jabberwocky' by Lewis Carroll.
- Prepare class performance for younger pupils.
- Produce definitions of invented nonsense words.
- Read 'The Magic Box' by Kit Wright.
- Write own version.
- Read 'The Secret' by Pie Corbett
- Write own version.
- Edit and write up both poems for performance and wall display.
- Select a favourite poem from class anthology and write a response.

You will notice that in this unit the poems read do not act as models for the children's writing. Whilst children should experience a broad diet of poetry reading, many of the forms they will meet are too hard for children to attempt to write themselves.

WRITING FORMS

If the form becomes dominant it can stultify the quality of the writing. For instance, I have seen a thousand haiku that are all three lines long and have 17 syllables but are lifeless, having nothing illuminating to say. This is because the child's attention has focused upon counting syllables rather than on the words and the experience.

So the form should not constrain. Simple structures for writing can act as a coat-hanger for the children's own ideas so that their writing is not just a pale imitation but brings into being something new. So, a well-chosen form will release the child from worrying about structure. Form should not interfere with creativity but should liberate it.

There are some poems that have an almost magical ability to stimulate fantastic writing. They act as catalysts to writing, saying 'Come on, you too can write'. They are invitations to creativity and have the ability to light the imagination. For instance, Kit Wright's 'The Magic Box' never fails. I would also mention the following that can be found in *The Works – Poems for Key Stage 2* (Macmillan, 2006):

- The door – Miroslav Holub
- A boy's head – Miroslav Holub
- Cat began – Andrew Matthews
- 14 ways of touching the Peter – George MacBeth
- The magical mouse – Kenneth Patchen
- I saw a peacock – anon
- A fistful of pacifists – David Kitchen
- My name is – Pauline Clarke
- You! – traditional – Igbo
- Go inside – Charles Simic
- 13 ways of looking at a blackbird – Wallace Stevens
- In a station of the metro – Ezra Pound
- Cat in the window – Brian Morse
- Clouds – Teddy Corbett
- This is just to say – William Carlos Williams
- The red wheelbarrow – Wiliam Carlos Williams
- The sound collector – Roger McGough
- A poem to be spoken quietly / Wings – Pie Corbett
- Listen – John Cotton
- Body sounds – Katya Haine
- The oldest girl in the world – Carol Ann Duffy
- Things to do at Sandpoint – 5th grade class, Sandpoint, Idaho
- Wind – Dionne Brand
- For Francesca – Helen Dunmore
- Small dawn song – Philip Gross
- Not only – Brian Patten
- Fog – Carl Sandburg
- Leaves – Ted Hughes
- Amulet – Ted Hughes
- To make a prairie – Emily Dickinson
- Mamma Dot – Fred D'Aguiar
- Yes – Adrian Mitchell

- Our street – Les Baynton
- Oath of friendship – Anon
- Playing a dazzler – James Berry
- In the time of the wolf – Gillian Clarke
- Curious craft – Philip Gross

What sorts of forms lend themselves as creative coat-hangers? Collage poems (sometimes described as 'list' or 'model' poems) – which use a repetitive phrase to open each line – can be very useful. The collage poem has a long tradition stretching from Walt Whitman back to many cultures' oral poems and texts such as the Bible. The ideal collage poem provides a form for the children to tag on their own ideas. The 'collage' would make sure that each line was fresh, adding something new to the cumulative picture. Where a repeated phrase is used to produce a sort of 'litany', this is known as 'anaphora'. It is used in many religious texts such as the Bible and in work by Shakespeare, Spenser, Walt Whitman, Allen Ginsberg through to Adrian Henri. As a writing device for children, it is liberating. It can be quite simple:

I like the sound of bacon sizzling in the pan.
I like the sound of crisps being crunched.

or quite challenging (opposite is my model and a year 6 pupil's):

The lines that lead . . .	The lines that lead.
The door of disasters, a dangerous doom.	The wire of weariness, a winding line.
The alley of agony, an antique ache.	The escalator of ebullience, an enthusiastic alleyway.
The passage of purity, a peaceful palm.	The route of realities, an imaginary road.
The lane of loneliness, a limping leash.	The sidewalk of secrets, hidden, secluded.
The window of wisdom, a whisper of wanting.	The passage of perfection, a positive way.
The route of silences, trapped in a stone.	The tightrope of tears, a tragic story.
The path of distances, long forgotten.	The door of danger, a daring place.
The rooftop of humour, an escape from misery.	The feather of feelings, a fearful bird.
Pie Corbett	*Katie, 10 yrs*

Children who find language a real challenge may need to use simple formats to release their creativity. For those who do not enjoy writing, lack a sense of success or struggle with transcriptional skills, the following points will help:

- Do plenty of short-burst writing so they develop confidence and success, rather than trying to tackle the marathon of a story.
- Provide very simple and strong scaffolds.
- Before children write, make lists of words and ideas with the children.
- Before they write, use shared writing so that they have been part of making up a 'class example' together.
- Initially, keep editing to a minimum.
- Publish.

- Praise – be enthusiastic about every little success.

Here are some simple list-poem ideas that work well:

I wish I was. . .	In this picture is. . .
I wish I could listen to. . .	In the dream world is. . .
I wish I could see. . .	Through the magic door I
It is a secret but. . .	found. . .
Can you see. . .	I travelled the world and
I remember. . .	saw. . .
On Monday I saw. . .	On the other side of the Moon
Tomorrow I promise to. . .	is. . .

The other key structure is completely open – free verse. It is where the children make a pattern upon the page with the words. The lines can be long, short or both. Ideally, free verse should not sound like chopped-up prose but flow with the underlying rhythm of speech – memorable speech. An over-clipped style may lack an inner regularity which a well-written poem usually possesses – even if the flow is broken for effect. Reading one's writing aloud can help the child to 'hear' whether it flows well. Below is an example of the shared writing from a year 5 class following a stormy night – and a child's poem from the lesson.

THE PLOUGHED FIELD

The icy wind shreds leaves,
like a thousand broken sparrow's wings,
scattered on the frosted fields.
Ridged ruts
scratch lino cuts in parallel lines.
The earth ripples;
holly in the hedgerows is hard as iron.
A few berries speckle the green scarlet.

Year 5 – shared writing on board

ICY BREATH

The wind crashes
with a piercing squeal
into the arched reeds
ripping the green
to pieces of thread.
Hair bellows out
as the wind cuts
into your face.
Fiercely,
it bends saplings,
shredding leaves,
throwing fragments
into the air.

Tim, 9 yrs

Other structures may be borrowed from poets, or invented, as long as they liberate the writing and neither constrain nor dominate. The national poetry progression suggests that the key forms for children's poetic writing are:

- collage or list poem
- free verse
- shape poems (free verse in a shape)
- short-patterned poems, for example haiku, cinquain or kennings
- borrow or invent own pattern, for example pairs of lines
- simple rhyming form, for example rap

It is worth noting that rhyme is too difficult for most children and generally leads to doggerel. A few simple formats and rapping can be fun but usually it is a skill that only the most gifted use effectively. Also, early attempts at syllabic poetry such as haiku might be best attempted without worrying about counting syllables so that the children can focus upon creating a simple word-snapshot. The principal forms are free verse and collage poems.

CHAPTER 3
Poetry warm-up games

GETTING THE WORDS FLOWING – WARMING UP THE MIND

I often start by playing a word association game – just to get the children generating words and ideas rapidly – a sort of linguistic mental gymnastics. I say a word and the children have one minute in which to jot down as many words as possible. Ideas that work well:

Bonfire
Snow
Storm. . . .

Then try the same thing using different objects or images. Now they are having to look and respond, generating rapidly words and ideas. Encourage them to look closely – like an artist – as if they were a microscope – and to jot down words, phrases, what it looks like or reminds them of.

The point of this game is to begin to establish the idea of 'brainstorming' – generating words and ideas to select from.

USING 'POWERFUL' WORDS

Provide the children with sentences that are dull and use weak language, e.g.

The cat went along the wall.

Children have to spot the weak words and change them – and can add in words. However, discuss the dangers of 'overwriting', and talk about the importance of making sure that if an adjective is used it adds something powerful, new and necessary. Aim for:

- powerful verbs ('crept' not 'went')
- necessary adjectives ('rusty letterbox' rather than 'red letterbox')
- precise nouns (e.g. 'Siamese' rather than 'cat')
- precise details.

NEW WORD COMBINATIONS

Push the children to try out new combinations – unexpected combinations. This could be done by making a list of 'things' (nouns), starting with a chosen letter, e.g.

Parrot
Pliers
Paint
Porpoise

Hide this list and then make a list of adjectives – random, but starting with a different letter, e.g.

Trembling
Tiny
Terrific
Tatty

(Dictionaries can help this activity – the secret though is to write the lists separately.) Once you have done both lists, bring them together, e.g.

A trembling parrot
A tiny pair of pliers
Terrific paint
A tatty porpoise

You can take this idea further by making a list of things to write about – an old lady, concrete, owl, blu-tack, car. Then try to pair each idea with the most unlikely adjective you can think of – something that really is completely impossible, e.g.

Crunchy old lady
Soft concrete
Syrupy owl
Merry blu-tack
Jealous car

Now match the nouns up with the most unlikely verbs, e.g.

The old lady breakdanced.
The concrete floated.
The owl saluted.
The blu-tack yodelled.
The car sneezed.

You can use someone's initials or car number-plates, for example, HBT could be:

Hairy banana terrifies.
Heavy Boris tickles.
Happy bears torment.

INVENTING SIMILES ('LIKE' OR 'AS')

This can be done by inventing whacky, exaggerated images, e.g.

As cross as a snarling wasp in a traffic jam
As slow as a snail stuck on superglue, etc.

Ban the obvious clichés – 'as thin as . . .' should not be followed by pin, air, paper, stick, rake. Encourage the children to seek something totally new, e.g.

As thin as a strand of hair from a tiger's tail, etc.

Try working from an object, image or something simple like a crescent moon – generate similes using 'like', for example, 'The Moon is like. . .'

an eyelash
a hump backed bridge
a clown's smile
a nursery rhyme boat, etc.

Push them beyond 'banana' which is very obvious and a good example of not 'sifting and fishing' for a new idea.

Show the children how to turn similes into metaphors, e.g.

The Moon is like an eyelash = the eyelash Moon

CRAZY SIMILES

Now move into crazy similes – just invent any old thing, the odder the better! For example, 'The Moon is like. . .'

a zebra in hot pants
a lorry on fire
a half chewed doughnut
the moment when you sneeze
a tortoise chattering its teeth

USING METAPHORS

Try playing the 'furniture game' just to loosen up the mind and tune into metaphorical thinking where one thing becomes another. I usually offer suggestions to get them going so everyone writes down 'he is', 'she is', 'you are' or 'I am'. Then I suggest various categories and give a short space for thinking (animal, nature, tiny object, character from a book, piece of furniture, colour, emotion, etc.).

You are a lazy lizard languishing.
You are a bud exploding in May.
You are a microchip buzzing with computerized thoughts.
You are the BFG striding across the Buckingham Palace lawn.
You are the colour yellow cowering in a fruit bowl.
You are anger trapped in a cage of its own making.

WHERE GOD IS FOUND

He is caught in anyone's fingers.
In spring, he bursts out with the flowers.
At night he watches us all.
He is sensed in the scent of a flower.
He is heard in the rushing of the cool wind
and the running of clear water.
He is the touch of dawn
and the coming of daylight.
He is brighter than the sun rising.
He is seen in a brilliant flash of light.
He is grasped in the gleam of a dancer's hair.
In the summer, his scent is of scarlet roses.
He is the taste of a chunk of chocolate.
He is heard in the swaying of apple trees in the wind
and in the crunch of a crisp apple.
He is seen in a mind.
He is held in the glint of a cat's eye.
In autumn, he falls with the crinkly leaves
and sways in the sharp wind.
He sounds like church bells ringing all over town.
In winter, he crunches like someone trudging in the snow.
He is the touch of a flower petal.
He is the sound of trumpets blowing in Heaven.
He is the rustle of reeds swaying in the wind.
He is in everyone and everything.

Anna, 8 yrs

SHE IS

She is the wind dancing in the air.
She is like a flower opening.
She is a silent sleep in the dark night.
She is a sunbeam through the trees' blossom.
She is the summer dream of my heart.
She is a voice singing in the darkness.
She is a hammer that hammers a nail.
She is like a stone that will not budge.
She is a book open and read.
She is the ear that hears into the future.
She is the hand that wrinkles with the years.
She is the poem reading its own mind.
She is the bird that sings on the wires.
She is the distance between your enemy and yourself.
She is the mumble of lips.
She is the moment of God.

Year 3 – Mr Corbett's class –
King Offa Junior School

CRAZY METAPHORS

Make a list of objects and use personification to turn them into a whacky Disney world, e.g.

In my Disney World –
The chairs tiptoe home, the clock wolf whistles at the Moon,
The books sprout wings and fly, the windows melt gently,
The tables crack jokes and the doors creak their knees like old men.

USING SOUND EFFECTS

Play a quick-fire alliterative game – this could begin by the teacher saying an animal and the children thinking of alliterative phrases or sentences, e.g. 'dog' – *a dirty dog dug a deep ditch deviously.*

Get the children collecting examples of alliteration, similes and metaphor, and inventing their own examples. Play around with inventing alliterative sentences starting from key words – animals or objects or feelings (whistle, ant, jealousy) – and go for unexpected combinations – the less obvious the better:

> The weary wild **whistle** woke wearily and whispered waspishly.
> The angry awesome **ant** alighted alarmingly.
> The generous joking **jealousy** jumped joyfully.

JANE CLARKE'S WARM-UP GAME

The writer Jane Clarke e-mailed me a game she often uses in schools. She calls the game, 'Delicious Dinners'.

> Hi Pie, I'm not sure what age group you're aiming at, but this works with KS1 and 2 as a poetry warm-up. It is a warm-up using alliteration/adjectives that can generate some startling images. Begin by asking class, 'What's your favourite food?' Then get them to add words that begin with the same letter. The only rule is that it has to be delicious (though if you're feeling strong, and/or know the class well, Disgusting Dinners is a lot of fun too), e.g.
> spaghetti – super, special, sunny, sparkling, surprise etc.
> jelly – jazzy, jumping, jolly, joyful etc.
> carrots – crispy, crunchy, cheerful, charming etc.
> pizza – pink, perfect, polar, pretty etc.
>
> All best,
> Jane

Jane's latest picture book is *Gilbert in Deep*, illustrated by Charles Fuge (Simon and Schuster, 2007). Her contact e-mail address for school visits (KS1 and 2 only) is jane@jane-clarke.co.uk

MAKE COLLECTIONS FROM READING

Get the children collecting examples of alliteration, similes and metaphor, and inventing their own crazy examples. Have a board for crazy ideas – use Post-it notes. Distinguish between clichés and dead metaphors, and fresh inventions.

WORD SWAPS

This is a great game to play. Ask the children to write rapidly for a minute or so – any topic will do. They then have to swap words over – nouns or verbs work well. For instance:

This evening I brushed my teeth, washed my hair and then read a book before falling asleep.

Might become –

This evening I read my teeth, watched my hair and then brushed a book before I washed the television.

THE BLINDFOLD GAME

What can the children hear when they are blindfolded?

Blindfolded, I heard –

The rushing of the clouds,
The sighing of the grass,
The spinning of the earth,
The cracking of the glass.

Blindfolded, I imagined that I saw –

The crumbling of the walls,
The silence of the stones,
The stubbornness of Earth,
The growing of the bones.

To get the rhyme in, the fourth one may have to be invented.

MAGNETIC POEMS

If you can afford it, purchase a set of 'Magnetic Poetry' (or you may be lucky and find that in your school someone has the magnetic version of *Breakthrough to Literacy*). This might just be left out for children to create sentences or unusual combinations, or provided for a pair of children to use as a treat. Over Christmas this year, I invented a little routine. The rules are: select a set number of nouns, adjectives and verbs. Place these in three columns, randomly, in the order: verb, adjective, noun. Bring the words together in threes – then add in any little words or polishings to create something with surreal fluency:

You can –
Investigate absurd junk,
Stroke psychedelic monuments
And waste soft glass.

You who weld that fiery experiment,
Create our blue masterpiece
To dazzle angry dust.

Imagine a glorious song
And observe the rigid silhouette.

NAMES FOR PETS

My mother once had a dog called 'Cum ear' – well, that was what it responded to, because she kept saying 'Come here'! The dog thought that was its name and would only respond to those words. My brothers and I tried inventing new names. What sort of names would it be interesting to name a dog or cat?

Possible new names for my dog
Detective
Be very brief
Rubber tyres
Trousers
Socks
Chinese tea
Last night it rained
Blue carpet
Cold drink
Cola

OVERHEARDS

Rapid lists of 'things my teacher/dad/mum/brother says' can be fun:

My mum says –
Keep that door shut.
You are not going out like that.
Is that room tidy?
It won't get done on its own.

But children can also become reporters who loiter in the playground and gather snatches of talk. These can then be listed.

PANDORA'S BOX

Bring in a special box. Inside the box place a series of cards with writing subjects written in bold lettering that can easily be read by the children from their seats. Good topics might include – *mirror, door, window, key, lock, glass, stone, rose, fire, bone, water, house, ring, candle, knife, clock, coin, purse.*

Hold up some of the cards and give the children a short time to select their topic, which they write at the top of the page they are using. Make a list on a board of possible lines to write, e.g.

> The . . . . . . looks like. . . . . .
> It reminds me of. . . . . .
> It makes me feel. . . . . .
> It sounds like. . . . . .
> It feels like. . . . . .
> It tastes of. . . . . .
> It seems to. . . . . .
> It can. . . . . .
> It will. . . . . .

If they get stuck on one phrase, miss it out. Anything goes – the ideas can be real or invented. Give a time limit to add pressure. Encourage playfulness. Here is an example about a pond:

> The pond looks like Cyclops's eye.
> It reminds me of cold places and summer holidays.
> It makes me feel secret.
> It sounds like silence or wavelets lapping.
> It feels like a polished, wet mirror.
> It tastes of mud.
> It seems to do nothing but is restless underneath.
> It can be used as a frogs' swimming pool.
> It can be used as a water skiing lake for mice.

ALPHABET GAME

In pairs, children take it in turns to think of the next letter in the alphabet – but instead of saying the letter, they have to say a word, e.g.

> Apple
> Braces
> Cradle

Double
Elephant

and so on.

CHANGE

I have tried playing this game in many different ways. The basic idea is that the players have to change a sentence. A simple idea is to provide a sentence on a board. Then give the class, say, three minutes to rewrite the sentence making a change each time. Changes may be simple additions or alterations of a more expansive sort:

It seemed like years before the bus came along.
It seemed like ages before the swan flew overhead.
It always seems as if the clocks have stopped before the bus arrives.
It always dreams as if it was asleep before the goldfish swam past.

SURPRISING SENTENCES

Try this as a class game. Begin by writing a sentence on the board, e.g. 'Melanie cooked the sausages.' Children then have to write a sentence in reply that makes the first one surprising, e.g. 'The sausages barked at Melanie.' This game can be played with pairs supplying each other with initial sentences, or solo.

LAST WORD – FIRST WORD

Ask the children to write a sentence. It can help to say, 'If you cannot think of anything just write "I saw a cat" – but I think that you'll all think of something more interesting.' That usually sparks some interesting sentences. Then tell them that the only rule to this game is that the next sentence has to start with the last word of the previous sentence, e.g.

Bob cycled to his friend's house.
House prices are large.
Large eggs are laid by ostriches.
Ostriches run very quickly.
Quickly, they made their way home.
Home is a shed for Bob.
Bob cycled to his friend's house.

In my example above, I have ended up where I began!

MAKING IT MUSICAL

A good poem should flow. Encourage children to listen to the sounds of poems, to try to catch the underlying beat that words and sentences have. To tune them up to listening, try quick-fire rhyming games. You say a word and the children have five seconds to jot down a word that rhymes, e.g. *pain, feel, fly, true, goal.* Try saying a phrase or sentence and ask them to chant the underlying rhythm. For instance, the name of the haulage company Eddie Stobart has a fairly thumping beat to it – dee dee do dar. Try clapping names and words to catch the beat.

When reading aloud, linger over words and savour them, but also keep listening for the musical pattern that underpins all language.

STRENGTHENING THE IMAGINATION

'Children nowadays don't have much imagination. . .they watch too much TV.' I guess that I've heard that old chestnut in staff rooms across the country. Of course, every teacher knows that the ability to imagine is important to both thinking and learning, but how do you strengthen the ability to imagine?

Imagination is the ability to think in the abstract, picturing what might happen; to create and connect items that are not actually present. A well-trained imagination can conjure up an image based on reality but may also playfully wander, creating new possibilities. Imaginative people can often understand how others might feel or envisage what might happen. It is important to remember that imagination and memory are inextricably linked – you cannot imagine what you do not know. Try imagining a new colour and you'll find it is impossible!

Key imaginative skills
- To re-imagine the past so that you can 'see' it clearly;
- To hold an image in your mind so that you can 'look' carefully at it;
- To connect different items, creating something new;
- To 'see' or 'daydream' what might happen.

Imagination is essential to enjoying reading – so that the reader can enter that secondary world and powerfully live the story. It is also just as important to writing creatively. Try playing these games to help strengthen children's ability to imagine. The games can be played as creative 'warm-ups'.

READ AND DRAW

Find a short passage from a poem that describes a person, place or event. Read it aloud and ask the children to draw what they see.

WHAT NEXT?

Read the opening from a story poem and ask the children to 'imagine' what might happen next – they can tell their partner or draw a mini cartoon to show what might happen.

BRING THE PICTURE ALIVE

On the interactive whiteboard show a photo or piece of art. The children then have to imagine that they are in the photo – on mini whiteboards they list what they can see or hear, what they might feel or think if they were actually there.

COMBINATION GAME

The teacher says an object or creature (e.g. 'tree') and the children have to see it in their mind. Now they add in some extra detail (e.g. 'a golden tree'). Prompt them to add in what it looks like, where it is, what is is doing. Then they turn to their partner and describe what they saw.

CRAZY CHANGES

Ask the children to see an object, place or creature. Then gradually add in changes, e.g. put something on top of it, change the colour, set it alight, make it talk, make it move. . .

HOLD IT

Provide an object or image. Get the children to look carefully at it, noticing detail. Then remove it and they should try to 're-see' it in their minds, jotting down words to describe the details. Move on from this by just giving the children a word to focus upon, e.g. 'cat'. Tell them to look carefully at it in their minds. They should hold it in their minds and rapidly jot down describing words, trying hard to notice the details.

GUIDED DAYDREAM

This game helps children to develop the ability to imagine pictures in their minds. Ask the class to settle quietly and be ready to concentrate. They should stare at some small detail in the room in a fixed manner and then you ask them to imagine a place that they know well – a room where they live. Ask them to look round the room. What is on the floor and the walls. Now look out of the window. What can you see?

Now tell them that someone is about to rush into the room and say something. Who is it? What do they say? Take this at a slow pace – using an even tone. After a short while, ask them to tell their partner where they were, what they noticed and what happened.

WHAT IF...

This is a fun game and easy enough to play. Provide a starting point – a word chosen at random from a book, a photo or piece of art. Then the children have to brainstorm as many 'what if's as possible.

WHAT IF...

the Mona Lisa –
began to sing like Kylie Minogue,
yawned loudly,
asked the way to the shops,
winked at me,
wrinkled her nose,
ate a double cheeseburger and fries,
took her dog for a walk,
went to live in Barnsley?

Without the ability to imagine, the world would be a duller place. Perhaps it is an ability that we ought to be developing so that children can relive their past, predict their future and enter other worlds of possibilities. Einstein valued the imagination above science, for he believed that 'imagination is more important than knowledge'. Knowledge is limited, and can always be found out, but it is the imagination that will bring about new discoveries, new technologies, new thinking. Without it we are lost.

CROSSING THE RIVER

This creative 'warm-up' was e-mailed to me by the wonderful poet Roger Stevens. If you haven't yet visited his excellent website Poetryzone (see Appendices page 175) then you must. Roger wrote:

> Tell the class that they are standing on the bank of a river. The river is as wide as the classroom. Ask them to suggest ways to get to the other side. As they make suggestions, write them on the board. At first you'll probably have obvious things – but persist, as before long much odder suggestions start to appear.
>
> This is a brainstorming session and you are encouraging the children to be as wild and imaginative as possible. If their idea will get them across the divide, that's fine.
>
> You should end up with 30 or 40 suggestions! These might range from: cross over by bridge, swim, go by boat, to these suggestions from a group of Year 7 writers in Battle, East Sussex:

> > Join a circus and borrow the clown's stilts.
> > Blow up a puffer fish with helium and float across.
> > Cross using a pair of ancient Greek winged sandals.
> > Cross the river by standing on the tongue of a whale.
> > Wait for a very cold day, then when the river freezes skate across.
> > Catch a lift with the Flying Monkeys.

> Discuss with your group or class the order of lines in a poem like this. They might like to put the obvious things first and the most crazy suggestion last. You might also discuss rhythm and rhyme. Would your poem lend itself to either?

Brainstorm ideas for a poem such as:

Ten ways to get out of doing homework (a popular
   suggestion)
Seventeen ways to climb over a wall
Eleven ways to help mum
Things to do when you're really bored

There are many poems written like this. You'll find some in
The Works series such as Ian Macmillan's 'Ten Things Found
in a Wizard's Pocket' and Allan Ahlberg's 'Things I Have Been
Doing Lately'.

Cheers!
Roger

Find Roger's own poetry in *Why Otters Don't Wear Socks*
(Macmillan Children's Books, 2007) and his anthology *The
Secret Life of Pants* (A&C Black, 2006). His excellent website is
a MUST, so visit it at: www.poetryzone.co.uk. Children can
post their poems on the poetryzone. His other website,
www.rabbitpress.com, is also useful – it is where people can
buy other work by Roger and a few fellow poets published in
small presses.

'13 THINGS TO DO WITH A RAINBOW'

Roger's workshop works wonderfully. I tried it out in
Nottinghamshire at a small school gathering of year 6 pupils
from seven different schools. I used it as a 'warm-up'. I
explained that I was standing at the edge of a river. How
many ways could they think of in ten minutes to cross over?
It started slowly with the obvious (find a boat). The ideas
really got going once I said, 'Oh, I've thought of an idea. I
could shrink myself, sit on a leaf and wait for an autumn gale
to blow me across!' This idea acted as a catalyst for new ideas
– we invented 57 in ten minutes! When the ideas slowed
down, I gave them a quick ten-second buzz in a pair to
generate more.

The idea reminded me of a poem by Dave Horner, '13 things to do with a rainbow', which begins:

Keep it for a skipping rope.
Throw it like a boomerang.
Put it on your head and wear it as a hair-band.

This would also make a good starter – and it led me into inventing other titles, e.g.

5 things to do with –
a moon, a sun, a star, a planet, a cloud, lightning, a rumble of thunder, an ocean.

5 ways to –
climb a mountain, get to school, keep the teacher happy, make a tree grow.

OPPOSITE PAIRS

Make lists of pairs of words that are opposites such as hot/cold. Make a list of hot words – match these with cold things, e.g.

Spicy icicle
Sweltering frost
Blazing snow
Frozen sunbeam
Frosty oven
Chilly flame
Cool furnace

CHAPTER 4
Poetry writing games

PASS THE POEM

Provide a simple 'opening' that could act as a starter for a list poem and everyone rapidly jots down a few ideas. This can be passed round the room with new ideas added on or pinned to a wall. These can be joined to create a whole-class poem. Here are a few starters to try:

List of possible playful poem ideas
- In this magical bag I found . . .
- I dreamed . . .
- In the clouds I saw . . .
- Listen, can you hear . . .?
- Come with me to an impossible world where . . .
- Through the window I saw . . .
- At the end of the rainbow I saw . . .
- In the crystal ball I saw . . .
- In a girl's/boy's head is . . .
- Trapped inside the marble is . . .
- In the cupboard of dreams is . . .
- In the future . . .
- I wish I could . . .
- If only . . .

INNOVATING ON NOTICES

I thought of this idea on a train journey to Wakefield when we were sitting in the middle of nowhere with the twilight descending and the inevitable apology over the tannoy. I noticed a couple of signs and just began swapping words over. This is what I jotted down:

YOUR GUARD IS HERE TO HELP

Your fox is here to help.
Your wolf is here to hinder.
Your hippo is here to dream.
Your pizza is here to surprise.
Your cloud is here to indulge.

Just below it I noticed another sign and wrote:

EMERGENCY ALARM BY ENTRANCE DOORS

Emergency dog by entrance doors.
Emergency cat by scarlet doors.
Emergency cake by starlight doors.
Emergency tunnel by willow doors.

Of course, I could also go on to change the words 'emergency' and 'doors'. Start collecting school signs and noticing signs in the locality. Use these as a basis for rapid innovation and word play.

BECOMING A WINTER

I was reading an educational document quickly and misread 'Becoming a Writer' as 'Becoming a Winter'. What would happen if you became a winter – or summer – or a dragon – or an iceberg? In a few minutes, jot down ideas perhaps using time connectives to help structure what happens, e.g.

BECOMING A WINTER

At first, I just noticed the cold,
Chilling my bones
Till I shuddered and shook.

Next, it was the scales of frost
That glittered in the sunlight.

Then came the day I woke
To find my eyes glazed over
Like frozen puddles.

Finally, the snow
Streaming behind me
Wherever I walked,
Leaving a trail of ghostly white.

At night I lay in bed
Colder than stone.
An iceberg locked
In the seas of winter.

RIDDLE GAME

As a warm-up to writing riddles, play a one-line game. Children invent a clue about an object to see who can guess what it is. An alternative is for children to work in a small group – each preparing a clue about the same object to see who can guess.

To make a clue, first decide on the subject, e.g. a mirror. Then think of other things it looks like, what it does, expressions and other ideas. Make a simple clue but remember to hide the subject.

I am glassy.
I am a glass eye.
I can see you.
I am like a window on the world.
Broken, I bring seven years of bad luck.

Once children are happy with a simple clue, move on to using
'I am. . .But. . .'.

I am icy as a puddle
But will not easily melt.

I can copy your every move
But am always quite still.

I am like an eye spying on you
But am totally silent.

JAPANESE LISTS

Sei Shonagon lived about a thousand years ago. She was a
lady-in-waiting at the court of the Japanese empress in the
tenth century and is considered to be one of the greatest
writers in Japanese literature. She wrote a remarkable 'pillow
book' in which she lists all the things that attracted,
displeased or caught her attention in her everyday life. This is
how she began:

> Lord Korechika brought the Empress a bundle of
> notebooks. 'What shall we do with them?' Her Majesty
> asked me. 'The Emperor has already made arrangements
> for copying the "Records of the historian".' 'Let me make
> them into a pillow,' I said. . .I now had a vast quantity of
> paper at my disposal, and I set about filling the notebooks
> with odd facts, stories from the past, and all sorts of other
> things, often including the most trivial material. On the
> whole, I concentrated on things and people that I found
> charming and splendid; my notes are also full of poems
> and observations on trees and plants, birds and insects.
> *The Pillow Book*, Sei Shonagon (Penguin Classics, 2006)

Many of the entries are lists. These could be used as a basis for quick listings:

Things that make one's heart beat faster
Things that arouse a fond memory of the past
Elegant things
Unsuitable things
Things that cannot be compared
Rare things
Splendid things
Depressing things
Hateful things
Annoying things
Embarrassing things
Surprising and distressing things
Things worth seeing
Things that should be short/large
Nothing annoys me so much as. . .
Pleasing things
Clouds
Things that fall from the sky

Things that give a hot feeling
Shameful things
Things that have lost their power
Awkward things
Things without merit
Outstandingly splendid things
Things that are unpleasant to see. . .
It is very annoying when. . .
The ways in which carpenters eat
Things that give a clean/unclean feeling
Adorable things
Presumptuous things
Squalid things
People who seem to suffer
Enviable people
Things that one is in a hurry to see or hear
It is delightful when. . .

Her list of poetic subjects included: *The capital city. Hail. Bamboo grass. The round-leaved violet. Water oats. Flat river boats. The mandarin duck. Lawns. The green vine. The pear tree.* (*The Pillow Book,* Sei Shonagon (Penguin Classics, 2006)).

The lists are often quite simply put.

ELEGANT THINGS

A white coat over a violet waistcoat.
Duck eggs.
Shaved ice mixed with liana syrup and put in a new silver
bowl. A rosary of rock crystal.
Wisteria blossom.
Plum blossoms covered with snow.
A pretty child eating strawberries.

Her writing is usually simple, clear and directly records what she saw or heard or tasted. It is worth noticing that good writing is not about using fancy words but selecting the right word. Often it is simple, straightforward language that carries the punch. This came to me recently when I was working with teachers and we were looking for a verb for a branch. They suggested 'protrudes and elongates. What's wrong with "sticks out?"' I asked. The point is that 'protrudes' tells you what the branch is doing but 'sticks out' shows you – it helps you see the branch in your mind. (There is also the added benefit of the play on the word 'sticks' which is a metaphor.) Look at this piece by Sei Shonagon – simple, beautiful clarity.

When crossing a river in bright moonlight, I love to see the water scatter in showers of crystal under the oxen's feet.
The Pillow Book, Sei Shonagon (Penguin Classics, 2006)

HOURS, DAYS, WEEKS, MONTHS AND YEARS

My children take great delight in telling me that I was born in the year of the rat! Actually, I think they just made that up but the Japanese do have interesting ways of naming time. Here are some invented ideas. Just give the children three minutes to make lists – some can be illustrated. Try using different animals, plants, weather conditions or places. It helps if you can think of unusual ideas, or be specific by naming well, e.g.

WATER ANIMAL HOURS

The hour of the hermit crab.
The hour of the Portuguese man of war.
The hour of the hammerhead shark.
The hour of the blue whale.

PLANT DAYS

The day of the flag iris.
The day of the primrose.
The day of the maple trees.
The day of the great redwood.

WEATHER WEEKS

The week of the snow storm.
The week of thunder.
The week of sun.
The week of hail.

PLACE YEARS

The year of the mountain range.
The year of the icy hilltop.
The year of the silted river.
The year of the deepest valley.

In one of my notebooks I made a list of the names given to Japanese months, dating back 1,000 years. Can the children tell which month is which? To create a modern set of new names for months that relates to where you live, ask the children to think of things that happen during different months:

Which month?	Japanese name	Pie's Gloucestershire months
	1. Sprouting month	1. Grey cloud month
	2. Clothes-line month	2. Primrose month
	3. Ever-growing month	3. Buds bursting month
	4. Pretty white bush month	4. Fool's month
	5. Rice growing month	5. Glider month
	6. Rain month	6. Tee Shirt month
	7. Poem writing month	7. Sail away month
	8. Leaf dying month	8. Long Day month
	9. Long night month	9. Storytelling month
	10. Gods absent month	10. Apple month
	11. Frosty month	11. Frosted Leaf month
	12. Final month	12. The Gift month

SILENCES

What sorts of silences and still moments are there? Make a list with the class of silent moments and things and times. Turn each idea into a simple poetic line. Use numbers to list ideas.

> First there is the silence of snow.
> Second there is the silence just after the teacher asks a difficult question.
> Third there is the silence found hiding in cupboards.
> Fourth there is the silence of sunlight lounging on hot roofs.
> Fifth there is the silence of dark sleep.

> First there is the stillness of mountains.
> Second there is the stillness of the pavement.
> Third there is the stillness of a table's leg.
> Fourth there is the stillness of the statue's face.
> Fifth there is the stillness of my grandad's memory.

QUICK-FIRE DESCRIPTION

Bring in an object that might interest or intrigue. Brainstorm ideas and words. On mini whiteboards give a few minutes for children to raid the bank of words or invent new ideas and write a quick-fire poem list. Try using: an old piece of bark, lighting a candle, looking at marbles, the back of your hand, feathers, leaf skeletons.

like lace/neatly threaded/like a map/or a starfish far from home/crinkled parchment/veins leading nowhere

THE PERSONIFICATION GAME

Bring in an object or make a list of things. Then make a second list of verbs that are 'things that humans do, e.g. giggle, yawn, sneeze, dream, whisper. Give the children several minutes to match the lists and invent other ideas to create personification.

The tables whispered.
The chairs coughed politely.
A pencil tiptoed away.
Two exercise books took some exercise!

QUIRKY QUESTIONS

Make a list of key question words – who, where, when, why, what, how, have you, did you, is it, can we, etc. Then use these to ask questions about animals, objects, feelings, memories, abstract ideas, colours, numbers or actions. Suppose we chose the word 'tunnel'.

> Who is hidden inside?
> Where will it end?
> When did you decide to travel undergrounds?
> Why is it hollow?
> What sleeps in there?
> How many bats hang out inside?

Of course, questions can be swapped over and interesting answers supplied. Remember that the answers will be most effective if they are surprising and unexpected!

TALKING TO TURNIPS

In many poems, poets talk to animals or inanimate objects as if they could understand. What would you say to your class novel? What would you say to a television? Make a list of subjects and give the children several minutes to question the world by asking questions.

> Book, what secrets do you hide between your pages?
> Sunlight, where did you spend last night?
> Television, do you ever get tired of making a din?
> Snail, where did you get that shell?
> Turnip, where did you get that ridiculous name?

EXCLAMATIONS

Sometimes in a poem you will want to sound indignant or outraged. Sometimes you might want to 'boss' something about or give it instructions. Choose a subject and then list some commands.

Stone – get up and do something!
Stone – get off that beach!
Stone – speak up!
Stone – you are cold hearted!

QUICK LIES

In a funny way all stories are lies – well, fabrications at least. Poets, too, are good liars. 'My Love is like a red red rose.' Pull the other one! Telling lies or fabrication or inventing impossibilities is playful – 'The moon is a beachball kicked into the night by a giant.' Find subjects to create impossibilities around. For instance, the Moon. All you have to do is think of the Moon's qualities and then invent the opposite or new things about it which are not true.

THREE THINGS YOU NEVER KNEW ABOUT THE MOON

The Moon is used as a car park by my next door neighbour.
In the morning it likes to have a bowl of Frosties.
In the evening the Moon relaxes in a sauna.

LET'S PRETEND

This idea is in the same realms as 'lying'. When my children were toddlers, they loved to say, 'Let's pretend. . .', and we would make something up or pretend we were at the shops. Use those words as a simple frame for inventing ideas rapidly.

Let's pretend we are trapped in a bubble.
Let's pretend we can talk to hedgehogs.
Let's pretend we can travel through a straw.
Let's pretend the school is eaten by a maggot!

SYNESTHESIA

Try writing poems in which you purposefully mix up the senses. It can help to have a list idea such as 'I can see' and use this as a coat-hanger for ideas. Begin by making a list of the senses to remind children. Then show them how to mix senses up.

I can see the sound of a train's clickety clack.
I can see the taste of lemon sizzling.
I can see the feel of a milk bottle's condensation.
I can see the scent of tarmac roasting.

I can hear the sight of snow smouldering.
I can hear the scent of vinegar on my chips.
I can hear the feel of a hot teaspoon.
I can hear the taste of ice cream screaming sweetly.

BOASTING

Let the children make a list of their best attributes – it is great for making yourself feel good, especially if you exaggerate. Think of all the things that you would like to be and then become them!

Pie Corbett
Is the lead singer in a boy band;
Has just won a million pounds;
Can leapfrog over houses;
Can eat twelve hot dogs in one sitting.

EXAGGERATE

Make a quick list with the children of everyday things that happen in the classroom, on the streets, in shops, at work, on the sea, in the air and at home. Then take some and exaggerate!

> The clock ticks like a thundercrash.
> The carpet is a desert.
> The sink is an ocean.
> The table stands higher than the Big Ben tower.
> The window is as wide as the night sky.

MAKING THE ORDINARY POETIC

Take something that is everyday and ordinary – in fact, make a list. Then choose one item such as a dishcloth or a window. Now try to look at it with the poet's eye. This might mean trying to use words to capture what it really is like – trying to unlock its secret spell – or play with the dishcloth by making it talk, or tell secrets about it.

> The dishcloth sits
> Like a sad grey octopus,
> Tentacles dangling
> Like a Rasta haircut
> Bedraggled by rain.

MAD COMPARISONS

If John Donne can suggest that two lovers are like the two tips of a compass then let's make up some mad comparisons ourselves. Make a list of possible subjects. These work well – eyes, pond, lake, tower, key, lock, Moon, Sun, stars, a ring. Now invent new ideas for what these are like in a few minutes.

> The Moon is like a band of merry thieves.
> A key is like a notebook of ideas.
> A tower is like a wheelbarrow of potatoes.

AUTOBIOGRAPHY

In a way all writing is about ourselves because our words reveal our thoughts and feelings. Try using your own life and memories as a source. Ask the children to share some memories – maybe things that happened when they first went to school. Give them time to talk about this in pairs and then listen to a few memories as a class. Now show the children how to take a simple memory and turn it into a short-burst writing idea by using 'I recall. . .'.

'I recall – playing with playdough in the sandpit and Miss Willet reading *We're Going on a Bear Hunt* to us.'

'I recall – holding my mum's hand as we waited to go into the big school.'

WORD PLAY

Make a list of everyday expressions and then take them literally.

Her eyes shot round the room – we ducked down!

Here are some expressions to play about with:

It's raining cats and dogs	It makes my mouth water
To lead a dog's life	Flogging a dead horse
Don't put all your eggs into one basket	Food for thought
	To let off steam
Teach your grandma to suck eggs	Bury your head in the sand
He was over the Moon	To spread your wings
Like a bull in a china shop	I'll make mincemeat of him
She had her head in the clouds	Once in a blue Moon
To be kept in the dark	It's plain sailing
It's like looking for a needle in a haystack	Keep your shirt on
	He tried to sponge off me

To let off steam
To have a frog in the throat
She drove me up the wall
Let's strike while the iron is hot
Storm in a teacup
To kill two birds with one stone
I saw stars
Thank your lucky stars
To strike lucky
In the soup
By the skin of my teeth
Let sleeping dogs lie
You are a sly dog
She is a snake in the grass
She bit my head off
To have a sweet tooth
Let's have a whip round
A ring of truth about it
He slammed the door in my face
To take under your wing
I was caught in the eye of the storm
Don't jump down my throat about
    it
Let's look on the sunny side
One in the eye

One-armed bandit
They flagged us down
We drew a blank
It is top-drawer quality
We should cut and run
Dead as a doornail
Sight for sore eyes
It is an eyesore
I have the key to the problem of
    killing time
He is the lollipop man
I am over the Moon
To throw cold water on something
To put your foot in it
Open your big mouth
Keep your eye on it
To let fly
Out of the frying pan and into the
    fire
Like a fish out of water
I'd like to pick a bone with you
Flat as a pancake
Sent off with a flea in the ear
A thorn in my side/flesh

A STORM IN A TEACUP

My mother liked to use expressions such as an 'odd kettle of fish'. This always intrigued me. I could actually see the storm in the teacup or a kettle stuffed with fish! There are many ways in which you could play with idioms. The teacup game is based on culinary items so make a list – plate, bowl, saucepan, kettle, teapot, mixing bowl, cake tin, biscuit barrel. Then make a list of weather conditions – storm, snow, rain, thunder, lightning, hail, typhoon, tsunami, etc. Then combine, using the same pattern as 'storm in a teacup'. Pretend that at night the kitchen comes alive, but the weather conditions are variable! These look good if the children illustrate their ideas:

In the night kitchen we had –
A storm in a teacup,
Lightning in a kettle,
Frost in a tooth mug,
Snowstorm in a pepper pot.

NEW SAYINGS

My mum's world was peppered with expressions. When she suspected us of mischief, she would say that she had 'smelt a rat' or that 'trouble was brewing'. Hers was a world interpreted by such linguistic patterns. Most of us know the game of turning the expression on its head and taking it seriously, e.g. I had my head in the clouds/it was wet and foggy.

Recently, I found a collection of Armenian expressions and tried using these with Year 7 children to invent new ones based on the old. I have paired up an Armenian expression with its partner invention made by one of the children.

The cat which wears gloves will catch not one mouse.
The snake who wears a hood will sting no prey.

A fly may tumble into a king's glass.
A flea may settle on the teacher's neck.

He who is too fond of swimming may well end up in the whale's gut.
He who is too fond of driving may end up beneath the lorry's wheel.

What is sport to the cat is death for the mouse.
What is fun for the dog is hard on the bone.

What we realised when doing these is that to write a good one you really have to think about what the original saying means. Here are some other Armenian sayings to try out:

Fish in the sea will fetch no price.
Gold shines in mud.
A lie has short legs.
A friend will look you in the eye, whilst an enemy will catch
    your foot's attention.
A starving man will eat the soft parts of a stone.
The wolf waits for a foggy day and the thief for a Moonless
    night.
A cut of the sword will heal, but not a cut of the tongue.
Not every cloud will bring rain.
It does not matter to a blind man if candles are expensive.
The fool's bread is found in the smart man's stomach.
The distant bell sounds sweet.

THE ROOM OF STARS

I think the poet Philip Gross suggested this game. There are
many possibilities. Split the class in two. One half has to rapidly
make a list of places, e.g. room, town, city, village, mountain,
river, star, Sun, kitchen, alleyway, lawn, garden, castle, etc. The
other half has to make a list of nouns and abstract nouns, e.g.
memories, love, doom, sparklers, curtains, sunsets, wisdom,
jealousy, disasters, grass, hedgerows, teapots, certainty, etc. Then
put children into pairs and ask them to match the words listed
exactly in the order they write them down, e.g.

The land of whispers
The room of memories
The town of love
The city of doom
The village of sparklers
The mountain of curtains
The river of sunsets
The star of wisdom
The sun of jealousy
The kitchen of disasters
The alleyway of grass
The lawn of hedgerows

> The garden of teapots
> The castle of certainty

As well as places, you could try vehicles, or 'the moment of. . .', or time, e.g. 'the day of. . .', 'the week of. . .', 'the month of. . .', 'the year of. . .'. You could leave this just as a list of surprising and interesting combinations. Interestingly, many seem to have a power of their own. Show the children how to take one of the ideas that seems to have promise and extend it. I find this easiest by focusing on one idea based around an abstract noun. For instance, if you take the 'kitchen of disasters', you could list all sorts of disasters, e.g.

The kitchen of disasters is where –
The kettle's spout melted,
The teapot shattered into splinters,
The fridge shivered all night,
The sink sunk!

The city of doom could be a list of things that have happened that are doom-laden. Try a different pattern by using 'in', e.g.

In the city of doom –
The streets are awash with dead starfish
And the windows have wept tears of ice.
The shops are empty as silence.

In the city of emptiness –
The streets are silent as snow.
Houses are hollow as bones.
The cars glide by with no-one driving them.
The train station is waiting for a train that will never arrive.
The traffic lights flicker for no-one.

THE QUEST FOR BEAUTY

Poets often come up with interesting definitions of poetry:

Ian McMillan – 'a poem is a city'
Charles Simic – a poem is 'three mismatched shoes at the entrance of a dark alley'
Les Murray – 'poetry is a zoo'
William Carlos Williams – poems are little 'word machines'

In a way, a poem is a quest for beauty. Poets try to startle the reader with something fresh and beautiful so that after reading the poem they will never be quite the same person again. Teachers can help children create new and beautiful views of the world – to make their world richer. What else is a poem? Make a list of playful or beautiful ideas.

> A poem is a quest for beauty.
> A poem is a silver speckle.
> A poem is the edge of a swan's wing.
> A poem is a light in the dark.
> A poem is an answer to misunderstanding.
> A poem is a cornflake.

POETRY DOORS

The writer Stephanie Strickland says that 'poems are words that take you to three kinds of doors: closed doors, secret doors, and doors you don't know are there' (from *Here Comes Everybody*, see Bibliography, page 180). Make a list of doors that poetry is. Just be inventive – have some fun. It doesn't have to make sense; indeed, logic and sense will probably lead to dull writing.

> Poetry is a closed door.
> Poetry is a secret door.
> Poetry is a door that you did not know was there.
> Poetry is a door of foxes, as a sly as sunlight.
> Poetry is a door of dreams, where thoughts hide.

Poetry is a door of disasters, where stories crumble.
Poetry is a door of kittens playing.

WHAT CAN A POEM DO?

The amazing thing about poems is that you can do anything
you like in them. So make a list:

In a poem you can –
Swing in the park,
Throw bread to the ducks,
Sleep in doorways,
Eat 21 types of ice cream
In one afternoon,
Make friends with Spiderman,
Play hopscotch,
Visit Euro Disney,
Count cars when you are bored.
All this and more
In a poem!

MAGPIES

I have often talked about how children need to 'magpie' ideas
and words – from their reading, from each other, from their
lives. Writers need to be on the lookout for material to use in the
writing – to be alert to the world and to raid its possibilities.
Where else does writing material come from? I suppose we can
look inside ourselves, but very often there is just a dark silence
in there. We have to use our best resource – our experience (real
and imagined – inner and outer) – and then manipulate it.
Anyway, the idea of the writer being a magpie gave me this
couplet:

The writer is a magpie
As he dips into other lives,
Selecting bright baubles.

I then began to wonder what other creatures we might be.

The writer is a lion,
Roaring from the sidelines,
Sleeping in the dusty sunlight.

The writer is an amoeba,
splitting cells, slowly multiplying ideas.

Continue the idea – the writer is. . .the poet is. . . the teacher is. . .the child is. . .the author is. . .the dreamer is. . .the artist is. . .

RULES

There are many ways to invent rules for playful games. You could use your own words – but in some ways it is easier to take a poem or piece of prose and apply a rule. For instance, you could have rules to decide:

- How many words or syllables per line.
- Which letters to enlarge
- Which words to miss out
- When to add a word in

Take this chunk from one of my stories:

At that moment, Yann heard a strange noise. Something was caught in the brambles beside the barn. It was a beautiful white horse. Yann calmed the horse down, pulled the brambles to one side and set the horse free.

To his amazement, the horse turned and spoke to him. 'Yann, I am King of the wild horses. For setting me free I can grant you one wish. Come back at midnight when the moon is high and tell me your heart's desire.' Then the horse shook its mane, turned and galloped away.

This might be rearranged as a poem using the following 'rules':

First, split the passage up so that you have only eight words per line. In this way the first two lines would read:

At that moment, Yann heard a strange noise.
Something was caught in the brambles beside the

Now enlarge the eighth letter:

At that m**O**ment, Yann heard a strange noise.
Somethi**n**g was caught in the brambles beside the

Now omit the fourth word in each line:

At that m**O**ment, heard a strange noise.
Somethi**n**g was caught the brambles beside the

Now add in an extra word after the sixth word:

At that m**O**ment, heard a strange crunching noise.
Somethi**n**g was caught the brambles beside herself the

Having played about with your rules, now complete the poem, by altering it to make surreal sense – where the meaning may be playful but the grammar works. This might mean re-inserting words or altering a previous change:

At that m**O**ment, she heard a strange crunching noise.

Somethi**n**g was caught in the brambles besides the silent stream where

There was a barn. It w**a**s beautiful; a white horse, sunlit. Yann

calmed t**h**e horse, pulled the brambles angrily down, and to

one side **a**nd let the horse free. Desperately and To

his amaz**e**ment, the barn turned and spoke English to

him. 'Yann **I**, King of the sunlit wild

spaces, am joyful. F**O**r setting my timber limbs free, I can easily grant

you one w**i**sh. Be back at midnight tonight when

the moon **i**s bright and tell me faithfully your

heart's d**e**sire.' Then the barn shook its wild mane,

turned a**n**d galloped.

WORD SWAP

Take a short poem or verse and swap words over, borrowing from another poem, a dictionary or a totally different text type.

> To see a world in a grain of sand
> And a heaven in a wild flower,
> Hold infinity in the palm of your hand
> And eternity in an hour.

This might become:

> To see a dove in a pinch of lies
> And a heat wave in a tiger's tooth.
> Hold a grave in the power of your eyes
> And a blackened crow in a bone's truth.

An alternative is to directly swap words within a poem. So, the first verse of Blake's 'The Tyger' now might become:

Forest tyger burning symmetry
In the hand of the bright
What immortal night or tyger
Could frame thy fearful eye.

Another possibility is to create your own procedure. You can swap verbs, nouns, adjectives or verbs for nouns, etc. Here I have tried swapping over each noun with the next:

My original	Swapping nouns over
Stars	Freckles
are to reach for,	are to reach for,
beautiful freckles of hope,	beautiful stars of speckles,
speckles on velvet,	hope on ships,
to steer ships,	to steer velvet,
to comfort those trapped in the darkness of their making,	to comfort those trapped in the wayward of their making,
to lead the wayward when the compass falters,	to lead the darkness when the day falters,
to remind us that the day is almost breaking,	to remind us that the compass is almost breaking,
dawn is just out – taking time to warm the other side of the world.	time is just out – taking dawn to warm the other world of the side.

My original	Swapping nouns over
Stars are for wishes.	Wishes are for stars.
Stars are tiny lights of hope, fireflies in the night, golden specs to gaze at, tin tacks on a dark cloth, studs glittering, sequins on a first party dress.	Lights are tiny stars of fireflies, hope in the specs, golden night to gaze at, tin cloth on a dark tack, sequins glittering, studs on a first party star.
Stars are our brightest and best, shards of hope to keep us going, marking the place, marking the seasons, giving us reasons	Dresses are our brightest and best, hope of shards to keep us going, marking the seasons, marking the place, giving us gazers
because somewhere out there	because somewhere out there
there are other star gazers gazing back.	there are other star reasons gazing back.

POETRY BITS

Take a poem. Cut two, three or four pieces out of the poem in different places. Put them together to make a new poem – fill in the spaces. For instance:

My original poem	New poem
Go Inside –	**Go** *Sea* **–**

a river as it noses by burrowing between banks, carving through stone.	*See the sea,* *Feel the water slip* *Between fingers and toes,*
Within it must be lonely; except for the constant chatter of stones rattling along; except for the slither of eels and the silver of fish.	*Listen to its watery kiss –* *Except for the crush* *And crash of the storm,* **except for the slither** **of eels and the silver of fish.**
Go inside – you might find the sky or the Moon or a fisherman's face staring back.	*Stare into its watery mirror,* *See the sea's grey eye* *Crumple your face;* *See the image of the sky* **or the Moon or a fisherman's face** **staring back.**
Inside, there's the rush of waterfalls and a wave's curve. Inside there's the imprint of a whale and the shadow of a shark.	*Beware* *Of the cold handshake* *Of the watery grave and* **the shadow of a shark.**
Go inside – at least it will wash away the day's dirt and some may be dazzled by its power.	*See the sea –* *Touch its soft hands –* **it may not be as cold** **as you fear.**
Go inside – it may not be as cold as you fear.	

TYPOS

A 'typo' is the term used to describe a typing mistake in a piece of written work. In this game, the teacher provides a poem or verse. The children then decide on the type of 'typo' to introduce, e.g. what it would look like if it was typed up by someone who swaps 's' for 'f' and 'e' for 'o'.

Original by Mary Coleridge	With typos
After St Augustine	*Aster Ft Auguftine*
Sunshine let it be or frost,	Funfhine let it be or sroft,
Storm or calm, as thou shalt choose;	Ftorm or calm, af thou fhalt choofe;
Though thine every gift were lost,	Though thine every gist were loft,
Thee thyself we could not lose.	Thee thyfels we could not lofe.

BUILD ON A POEM

Take a short poem and copy it for the children. They then have to alter the poem by adding to it. This could be by adding in extra words, phrases or clauses. They could add in similes or extend each line. The idea is to produce something new, using something already created as a basis. Take this nursery rhyme.

Original	Adding in alliterative adjectives
Little Tommy Tittlemouse	Little terror Tommy Tittlemouse
lived in a little house;	lived in a little hairy house;
he caught fishes	he caught floury fishes
in other men's ditches.	in other men's dirty ditches.

The children could create a rule for themselves. For instance, add in a new word or phrase every two words, or insert a new line between each line or a simile for each noun:

New word every two words	Alternate new lines	Similes
Little Tommy Trotty Tittlemouse lived in side a little happy house; he caught forty fishes in other old men's ditches.	Little Tommy Tittlemouse had many dreams, lived in a little house; made many schemes he caught fishes instead of wishes in other men's ditches.	Little Tommy Tittlemouse Like an elf lived in a little house, as high as a shelf; he caught fishes as gold as a bell. in other men's ditches as deep as a well.

MESOSTICS

A mesostic is an acrostic except the key letters are used within the lines. Again, you could have a rule (every tenth letter) or just begin by writing the topic down the centre of the page and then build a poem around it:

ANIMAL RIDDLE

like a small **B**ear
bundles over the dark road,
brushes p**A**st the front gate,
as if she owns the joint.
rolls the **D**ustbin,
like an expert barrel rider,
tucks into yesterday's **G**arbage,
crunches worms for titbits.
wakes us from d**E**ep sleep,
blinks back at torchlight.
our midnight feaste**R**,
ghost-friend,
moon-lit
zebra-bear.

THE SIMILE GAME

Look at the list of common similes below and ask the children to explain to their partner the story behind the simile. Try inventing new similes and listing them. Collect the best from scanning poems and novels. Make class lists. Discuss why a simile works – is it just a visual similarity? Create a simile alphabet in pairs or small groups within a few minutes.

As brave as a lion
As busy as a cat on a hot tin roof
As cunning as a fox
As deaf as a post
As dry as dust
As happy as Larry
As happy as a rat with a gold tooth
As hungry as a bear
As hungry as a wolf
As innocent as a lamb
As mad as a hatter
As patient as Job
As poor as a church mouse
As proud as a peacock
As scarce as hen's teeth
As silly as a goose
As slippery as an eel
As slow as a tortoise
As sly as a fox
As stubborn as a mule
As thin as a toothpick
As timid as a rabbit
As tricky as a box of monkeys
As welcome as a skunk at a lawn party
As wise as Solomon

DEAD METAPHORS

Dead metaphors are clichés – they are the ones that everyone knows and have been used so many times that they are just a part of everyday language, e.g.

Stone cold
A heart of stone
Apple of my eye
Boiling mad
Steer clear
Bear fruit
Hatch a plan
Difficult to swallow

Of course, the first time these were used they would have been arresting – something new and apt. Now they have become stale and have little fresh impact. Collect as many as possible from reading and noticing each other's speech. Make a list. Use these for a writing game by taking them literally, e.g.

I felt stone cold –
My arms were rock
And my legs were granite.

She was the apple of my eye –
But someone took a bite
Out of my sight!

My teacher was boiling mad –
Steam came out of her mouth!

I hatched a plan –
It is only just able to walk
And needs bottle feeding daily.

This sort of language play helps children look anew at language that they may just be using without really thinking about its meaning.

INVENTING METAPHORS

First of all, identify something that you want to create a metaphor around – for instance the stars. Now think of something that is like the subject or something to do with the subject – they shine, glitter, are like tin tacks, like diamonds, like jewels, like fiery eyes. Now use an idea to make a metaphor, remembering not to use the word 'like', e.g.

> The stars are shiny glitter.
> The stars tin tacked to the night.
> The diamond stars shine.
> The jewelled stars.
> The fiery stars eyed the world.

A simple way to invent a metaphor is to:

a. Generate a simile – the stars are like diamonds.
b. Omit the word 'like' – the stars are diamonds.
c. Move the noun in front of the image – the diamond stars.

Dylan Thomas used this technique in his writing.

EXTENDING THE METAPHOR

This is much easier than you may imagine. Take a simple simile, e.g.

> My teacher is like an eagle.

Turn this into a metaphor by removing the word like. Now think about what eagles do and just extend the sentence further, e.g.

> My teacher is an eagle swooping around the room, hovering over his students, diving down on innocent prey and demolishing them with the terrible grip of his talons.

THE WORD WAITER

Brian Moses once wrote a poem that involved a 'word waiter' who could serve up only a certain number of words. This can be used for short-burst writing, haiku, letters or news items. The randomness of the selection adds a challenging edge that often forces creativity beyond the predictable. The word waiter might serve up a character, place and dilemma for storytelling. Here are some possible starters – but ask the children and add many more ingredients!

Object	Verb	comparison
Spoon	Giggle	Nail
Raindrop	Comb	Chestnut
Car	Sneeze	Sawdust
Mirror	Cascade	Sunlight
Key	Burn	Tissue
Tower	Act	Leaves
Apple	Explain	Handbag
Smile	Sleep	Robin's eye

e.g.

The spoon slept as quiet as sunlight.
The raindrop sneezed like sawdust falling.

DREAM JARS

In *Gulliver's Travels* (Swift, Penguin Classics, 1994) there is a good description of what he has in his pockets. This idea led into making lists of the contents of Mrs Thatcher's handbag and I seem to recall that one witty lad wrote a list of what was found in Emu's beak – Michael Parkinson's finger! Other stories often lend themselves to writing ideas. *The BFG* (Dahl, Puffin, 2007) can be used to create dream jars. You could write about the contents or how to use them.

In the red nightmare jar –
Is a drop of blood from the sword that killed St Thomas,
Is a drop of paint from the letterbox in King's Lane,
Is a traffic light's eye from the High Street,
Is a red card from the referee's collection.

THE TROUT FISHING GAME

This game came from an idea in a poem by Richard Brautigan (author of the novel *Trout Fishing in America*) that I have adapted. To play the game, make a long list of possible subjects for writing, e.g. *worries, bicycles, recipes, trout, clouds, bees.* Choose one or two to work on as a class. Decide whether the subject is beautiful or ugly and write your opening line using this pattern:

A bee is not a beautiful thing.

Now make a list of contrasting subjects, using the following pattern:

A bee is not a beautiful thing;
It's not like a kingfisher
Hurrying in its flashy coat of blues and scarlet.
It's not like a dandelion
Shaking its golden mane.
It's not like a Siamese cat's eyes
Of Egyptian sapphire.

THE DRAGON CUTTER

Another idea that came from reading Richard Brautigan involved the idea of someone having a job as a 'dragon cutter'. This got me thinking about possible jobs that might only be found in fairy tales such as:

Ogre wedding planner	Crown settler	Web poet
Dwarf grabber	Rainbow singer	Troll weaver
Unicorn polisher	Dawn teller	Mirror dreamer
Medusa netter	Spider planter	Apple nurse
Stone fisher	Needle philosopher	Heart healer
Cloak hunter	Spinning wheel scientist	Tower carrier
Orc skimmer	Cave farmer	Bridge trickster
Ring breather	Bear writer	Riddle snatcher
Glass mountain polisher	Golden hen watchsmith	Ash tutor
Iron shoe soothsayer	Talking harp storyteller	Well printer

Of course, children could be asked to invent other jobs. More interesting would be definitions – what do these people do? You could invent a repeating pattern, e.g.

In the land of dragons,
The dwarf grabber waits by the old tin mine.

In the land of dragons,
The stone fisher sits on the mountainside,
Waiting with his metal net,
for a stone to move.

In the land of dragons,
The ring breather
Waits by the old phone,
Inhaling gold dust.

Or show the children how to take an idea and follow it through, e.g.

The bridge trickster
Waits by the river,
Detecting invisible bridges
And making sure
The stone does not crumble.

She casts a bridge
Across impassable valleys;
The King demands
A glittering arc of colour.

The bridge trickster,
Throws raindrops at the sun.

It is worth checking out Brautigan's poetry as a source for poetry ideas. He has a quirky turn of mind that appeals to children. See the website (teachers only): http://www.brautigan.net/poetry.html #unpublished

A NUISANCE OF NOUNS

Ask the children to explain the collective nouns in the alphabet below and then create their own alphabet – this might best be done in small teams, dividing the alphabet up between them.

An abandonment of orphans
A ballet dance of swans
A crush of rhinoceroses
A dose of doctors
An elephant of enormities
A fidget of school children
A glacier of fridges
A hover of hawks
An inquisition of judges
A Jonah of shipwrecks
A knuckle of robbers
A lottery of dice
A misery of bullets
A number of mathematicians
An outrage of stars
A prayer of nuns
A quake of cowards

A roundabout of arguments
A swelter of duvets
A tangle of tricksters
An upset of horoscopes
A vein of goldfinch
A wonder of stars
An x-ray of soothsayers
A zeal of enthusiasts

TIGERS IN RED WEATHER

There is a great idea in a Wallace Stevens' poem 'Disillusionment of Ten O'Clock' in which he envisages a sailor who is dreaming of trapping 'tigers in red weather'. This made me think about what else might be lurking in people's minds. Start with an explorer's dreams:

'An explorer is dreaming of. . .'

Then generate what he might be dreaming about – try to think of something exotic that can only be found in far off and extraordinary places. Part of the answer to doing this, may be in helping the children to think of a distant place (either from holiday or TV programme) and then an exotic detail – something that is different:

'An explorer dreams of
a white egret standing still
in the shallows of the Nile.'

Of course, you use just invented ideas:

A traveller dreams of:
The starlight scattered like glittering dust,
The suction of a black hole,
The pulse of a purple star,
The asteroid storm like so many giant crumbs,
The glimmer of new life struggling,
The weightless darkness
And eternity's deaf silences.

MAKING BUTTERFLIES OUT OF LIONS

Charles Bukowski is definitely not a child's author though I have one idea of his that is very memorable and gave me a little game which involves inventing creatures. The idea is to make a creature out of another creature. For instance:

You cannot make a tiger
Out of a moth
But you can make a Chinese lantern.

You cannot make a tiger
Out of a moth
But you can make a sunflower's petals.

Then I began to try out other creatures, trying to match up the most unlikely combinations and contrasts:

You cannot make a whale
Out of a parrot
But you can make a rainbow.

You cannot make a wolf
Out of an electric eel
But you can make a nasty shock!

Try listing two columns of animals – big, bold and fierce ones, then smaller and more surprising ones to use as contrasts. Think of domestic, farm, wild creatures and ones that inhabit the sky or sea or live underground.

THE ALPHABET GAME

Most teachers have a few alphabet games up their sleeves. This is a new one that came to me one day as I was flicking through the dictionary, idly wondering what could be done. I alighted on the letter B and wrote down a list of B words that I might use to start off sentences, all of them nouns – birdtable, bride, biscuit, bun, bath, bag and birthday. I wrote these down the left-hand side of the page and timed myself – one minute to see what I could write – a sentence for each one. You can use plurals. Ready, steady – GO!

Birdtable with a kingfisher.
Brides like swans or meringues.
Biscuits like small brown wheels.
Buns for munching.
Bags in a supermarket patiently wait to bulge.
Birthdays blossom.

I was aiming to make each one special. I tried to use a simile or an unusual angle.

AN ALPHABET OF THINGS

Use a dictionary. Make a list of things, e.g. Ape, Bear, Custard, Door. Then find an adjective that would not normally be used and is surprising. Create the list, e.g.

The antique ape
The business bear
The cruel custard
The disappointed door

This could be extended to include an unlikely verb as well, e.g.

> The antique ape argued.
> The business-like bear burst.
> The cruel custard calmed.
> The disappointed door drooped.

THE IRON EYE

Tristan Tzara has an opening line that has always struck me. It is about an iron eye changing into gold. I suppose I am drawn to the idea of transformations. What might transform into what? I thought of using the word 'therefore' to act as a link:

> The purring fingernail will change to butterflies
> Therefore
> The electric butter will change to rooftops.

The rules for the game are that you have to use an unexpected and impossible adjective for the first noun (purring fingernail) and then what it changes into has to be a total surprise. The idea is to shake off anything that is at all predictable or clichéd. It can help to list plenty of nouns – things that could be changed. Then another collection of ideas of what they might be changed into. Finally, a list of very varied adjectives.

> The purring fingernail will change to butterflies
> Therefore
> The electric butter will change to rooftops
> Therefore
> The patient toenail will change to sunlight
> Therefore
> The noisy teabag will change to a thank you
> Therefore
> The tired ocean will change to text messages.

Tristan Tzara, writing about Dadaism, stated:

What we want now is spontaneity. Not because it is better or
more beautiful than anything else. But because everything
that issues freely from ourselves, without the intervention of
speculative ideas, represents us. We must intensify this
quantity of life that readily spends itself in every quarter. Art is
not the most precious manifestation of life. Art has not the
celestial and universal value that people like to attribute to it.
Life is far more interesting . . . Dada covers things with an
artificial gentleness, a snow of butterflies released from the
head of a prestidigitator.

in Motherwell, *The Dada Painters and Poets*,
Harvard University Press, 1989

That last line gave me another poetry idea. Swap the word
'prestidigitator' for 'magician'. What else might be trapped
under a magician's hat – or what might be tugged from the
hat or hidden in a magician's cabinet? Work with the class to
invent a pattern – or several patterns, e.g.

Out of the magician's hat –
A snow of butterflies flows.

Out of the magician's hat –
A surprised rabbit's ears appear.

Out of the magician's hat –
A pineapple bristling yellow and green.

Out of the magician's hat –
A pair of ladies in sequinned tights wriggle free.

Try showing how one idea might be extended by just thinking
what would happen next, e.g.

> Out of the magician's hat –
> A snow of butterflies flows,
> Wings flickering
> As they pour out
> Like white, frail smoke,
> Fragile petals
> Scattering across the audience,
> Alighting on an elegant shoulder
> Or a bald man's shiny head.

THE LOST PHONE

Bring in a mobile phone (or any other object of interest). Tell the children that you found it. To whom does it belong? Make a list – be as extravagant as you wish. Think of characters from books, films, TV, computer games, mythology, traditional tales, politics, famous people. . .

> I wonder whose mobile phone this is?
> Perhaps it belongs to –
> Superman's nan,
> Mrs Bigalow from the corner shop,
> Gordon Brown's aunty,
> Paddington Bear's long-lost sister,
> George Bush's lapdog,
> Medusa's uncle,
> The bloke from the garage with orange hair. . .

NURSERY RHYMES

Select three or four nursery rhymes. Cut them up line by line. Reselect lines and create a new rhyme – create extra lines to complete where necessary.

PREPOSITION POEM

This could be based on a scene that you are looking at – or an imaginary world. Collect some preposition words – explaining that they are words that tell us the 'position' of things – above, below, beside, inside, outside, under, beyond, etc. Then use these to open each line. Try asking the children to look at something very small that no-one else will have noticed and then use this as a starting point. For instance, I can see some paint peeling on the radiator. This might give me:

> Above the peeling paint is a grill of heat.
> Behind the peeling paint is darkness as yet unseen.
> In front of the peeling paint is a current of invisible air.
> Under the peeling paint is the desert of carpet.

Notice the pattern – preposition + item + is. Try also imaginary landscapes (it may help to list possible places). Notice the difference in the pattern:

> Above the glass mountain, a sunset splinters.
> Behind the castle of fire, a wolf howls.
> In front of the waterfall, a silver salmon leaps.
> Under the forest floor, the badger's set.

THE GLASS TOWER IN MY DREAM

Years ago I had a dream about travelling at night in a strange world. Much of the landscape was on fire. In the end I came to a tall tower made of glass or some sort of crystal. You could see all the people living in the tower and the staircases spiralling up and down. The tower was a place of refuge from the devastation below. Begin this idea by listing with the children places – tower, cage, prison, palace, cathedral, hut, dungeon, etc. Then generate a list of characters – hero, heroine, thief, judge, master, captain, follower, priest, soldier, sailor, villain, brigand, angel. . . Use my pattern to create a picture of who was in the tower of my dream – who did you 'see' and what did you 'hear'?

> In the crystal tower of my dreams,
> I saw the priest laughing.
>
> In the glass cage of my dreams,
> I saw the hero dancing.
>
> In the crystal prison of my dreams,
> I heard the captain telling a lie.
>
> In the glass palace of my dreams,
> I heard the princess weeping tears like beads.

MIRRORS

I once bought a special mirror. The edges are made of fragments of pottery. If you look closely you can see: a Buddha, a hare, a cathedral, a violin, a fish leaping and many other interesting images set around the glass. Children have always been interested in the mirror. This gave me an interesting idea. Suppose you had a mirror made of fishes – what would you see in it? Suppose the mirror was made of a violin, or a hare.

> Inside the mirror of fishes,
> A trout glitters.
>
> Inside the mirror of hares,
> The joker boxes.
>
> Inside the mirror of sunsets,
> A rainbow's scarlet face.
>
> Inside the mirror of buses,
> The timetable of hope.
>
> Inside the mirror of night,
> A dark mouth opening.

MAKING FRIENDS

As a child I was always trying to make friends with different animals – dogs and cats, of course, but if I thought I had a chance with any creature I was there, talking to it like some long-lost friend. I kept spiders and worms as pets! So what would you need to do to make friends with any creature? Make a list of animals that would make interesting pets. Choose animals that you know about, and think about what they like doing:

> To make friends with a dog,
> Try barking, scratching your hind quarters and digging up
> bones.
>
> To make friends with a cat,
> Try curling up like a question-mark, purring and eating fish.

CHANGES

Children know many stories that involve transformations – from *Beauty and the Beast* to *The Ugly Duckling* to *Vampires, Frankenstein* and *Spiderman*. With the children, make a list of objects or creatures and transform them. Use this pattern or invent your own:

> The tiger becomes
> a wooden bench.

Of course, it can be more interesting if you select slightly unusual creatures or objects.

> The snow leopard becomes
> a cup of sweet mint tea.

It might be worth trying to link the creature and what it becomes. In some way there has to be a connection – the colour, perhaps, should be similar.

The tiger becomes
a sunset growling.

The snow leopard becomes
a speckled Persian carpet.

ADVERTS ON THE UNDERGROUND

While sitting on the tube recently I noticed several new
poetry ideas – in adverts. The first one I call 'mistakes' and is
based on an advert for the Bridget Jones film in which she
regrets having asked one of the characters into her life. I
decided that it might be interesting to list 'regrets' or
'mistakes'.

I think I may have made a mistake –
hiding the last fruit gum in the cat's bowl,
putting a cactus on the teacher's chair,
slipping a banana skin under an elephant's foot. . .

The other advert must have been for a hotel. It ran something
like this: 'Hands up those who fancy two nights for the price
of one.' The writing idea is to make a list of other things you
fancy, e.g.

Hands up who fancies –
A trip to the other side of the Moon,
A hot dog,
A holiday in Honolulu,
A trip to Orlando,
A Mars bar in batter.

WORD PLAY

This game involves collecting words that might have different meanings. Take the word 'aftermath'. The dictionary will tell you that this means, 'the consequences of an event or action'. However, to a child this might be 'what happens after mathematics finishes'. Here are some other words that make a useful source for new definitions:

Blindfold	Earwig	Kidnap
Bugbear	Eavesdrop	Nightmare
Butterfly	Foxglove	Perfume
Cartoon	Cowslip	Sandwich
Deadline	Handicap	Starboard

POETRY TREASURE TRAIL

Each child has to bring back an object or photo of something that they have seen – object, creature, something natural, an overheard snippet, an event. . .

You could then use a simple framework to create a poem. Begin by working on a group poem with the teacher scribing, taking and challenging their ideas. Take the object. Then invent ideas:

I found it. . .
It is made of. . .
If let loose, it can. . .
It dreams of. . .
If you saw it you would. . .

Here is an example. . .

THE CORKSCREW

I found it wandering
At the edge of the cutlery drawer,
Silvery hands in its pockets and its sharp nose
Sniffing the wind.

It is made of butter
And the lies of little ones,
Of sunlight and the twist
At the end of a murder mystery.

If let loose, it can bask
All day like a shark
Waiting in the shallows
Or queue up at Tescos
And argue with the girl
On the till,
Bored by too many customers' complaints.

It dreams of
Sunsets and little birds,
Of sadness wrapped in fur
And salt on the tongue tip.

If you saw it, you would
Giggle and then hand it back
Without a whisper,
In return for a free Mars bar
And a planet for your pocket
To keep you warm and giddy
As you bicycle home.

CHAPTER 5

Reading workshop ideas

My main intention with reading poetry is to provide something that will remain in everyone's memory and living imagination as an experience that will burn like a metaphor forever. The poem is there to be experienced. Poems are not like sums – you cannot always explain what they mean – but the words may move you.

When looking at worthwhile poems – poems that have some sort of bite – our aim should be to develop a love for the poem, an intimacy between the child's imagination and the words.

There are many poems that are easy to understand and lightweight that will be fun to read and chant but I've always been more interested in presenting poems that will actually influence the imagination – poems that will reconstruct the brain and make it one room larger. Kafka said that, 'one should only read books which bite and sting. . . if the book we are reading does not wake us up with a blow to the head, what's the point in reading? A book must be the axe which smashes the frozen sea within us.'

> A book must be the axe
> Which smashes the frozen sea within us.
>
> A book must be the flame
> That burns inside the mind forever.

The point about challenging poetry is that it does not have to be fully understood – it is there to be experienced. Children will not have the critical language let alone faculties to be able to discuss Shakespeare in any depth, but they can experience it, and often link into a true sense of the poem's intentions. What has to be avoided is strapping the poem to a chair and trying to thrash a meaning out of it! Too many lessons about poetry are about spotting verbs rather than deepening understanding and appreciation. Here are some poetry reading and writing ideas based around familiar and great poems. These should give you a feel for the sort of activities that you might use for any poem.

'THE TYGER'

There is a fabulous reading of this poem by John Agard and you will find it on the CD *Poems Out Loud*, edited by Brian Moses. This is an essential buy even if for just this one reading. I have known teachers cry when hearing it – one lady in Bromley said it 'sounded like the earth was speaking to me'. The point about poetry is that it is not just words upon the page – it is also about sound, in the same way that music is about sounds – and to explain how sound works is not easy! We can discuss the meaning of the words but to explain how the conjunction between the words and the sounds works upon us is almost impossible.

So, I would begin by reading the poem aloud – or playing John Agard's reading, if possible. Maybe listen a few times, then ask the children to jot down responses and share. What does it remind them of or make them think about? What is the most memorable image in the poem? Have they ever wanted to talk to an animal?

Bring the poem alive in different ways:

- One interesting way into this poem is to copy it and cut it up line by line. Give different groups different verses and ask them to put the lines together in the order that they think the poet had. Follow this with the children reading in groups.

- Now listen to John Agard's reading several times. On the second time ask them to jot down notes – thoughts, ideas, questions, key words, etc.
- Look at a coloured photo or video (google image) of a tiger. Brainstorm words and ideas – discuss lists.
- Which words – choose only two – go best with a tiger – mystery, magic, fierce, hot, orange, striped, pacing, glaring, eyes, cruel, jagged, intense, calm, soft, velvet? Now choose three words from the poem that best reflect the feeling of the poem. Discuss choices.
- It is worth telling the children that Blake had never seen a tiger!
- In groups, prepare a reading of the poem.
- Set the reading to music or sound effects.
- One interesting activity is to ask each group to read in different ways. For instance, you could have: rap reading, slow reading, sing it, read with percussion, read with simple chime bars, read varying girl and boy voices.
- Discuss which reading suited the poem best and why.
- Innovate on the line 'in the forest of the night', e.g. in the cities of the day, in the city of the sun, in the forest of the Moon, etc.
- Read through each verse – pause and discuss – listen to children's ideas. Even the stranger responses show that a child is struggling to understand.
- Ask the children to raise questions about the poem.
- Look at images of a blacksmith at work and relate them to the fourth verse – who is the blacksmith and what is he making?
- Discuss in pairs who the 'he' in the poem might be.
- Sort these ideas into numerical order in which 1 is the one you most agree with. This poem is about:
  - tigers
  - a blacksmith
  - making animals
  - creating things
  - the imagination
  - imagining and creating works of art
  - God creating the world

rkshop ideas

- wondering how things got to be the way they are
- Discuss:
  - How does the tiger feel?
  - How does the being that made the tiger feel?
  - How does the poem make you feel?
  - What is the being like – what can he do?
  - Where did the materials come from to make the tiger? How was it done?
- Try imitating the question idea by writing a new poem. Choose a mythic creature such as a wolf, eagle, hawk, crow, lion, serpent or owl – and ask it questions.

'JABBERWOCKY'

I have always loved this poem – possibly because my parents read it to me as a child. I didn't understand it at all but I loved the rhythm and the drama and the strange language.

This is a great poem for performance. The children should work in groups and prepare a dramatic reading with a chorus, the father and son. They need to think carefully about how to vary the volume, pace and expression – and also use background sounds. If they can, images on the interactive whiteboard would also add to the impact. It would make an ideal class performance. Here are some other ideas:

- Hot seat the father.
- Interview, in role as journalists, the son.
- Prepare a news bulletin about what has happened.
- Write up as news items for local paper.
- Write definitions of the different creatures mentioned, e.g. slithy toves, jubjub bird, bandersnatch, e.g. 'The Bandersnatch is a shy creature that is rarely seen. If disturbed, it may attack humans. . .'
- Make a list of invented words and in pairs try to work out what they mean.
- Present the poem as a cloze procedure with some of the nonsense words missing and ask children to complete with real words.

- Invent five new nonsense words and swap with a partner who has to use them to write several sentences.
- Create a poster warning locals of such dangerous creatures.
- Write five ways to trap a bandersnatch or jabberwocky.
- Describe the life cycle of one of the creatures with illustrations.
- Hold a class debate – or put father and son on trial. Should the jabberwocky have been killed (it was a rare species)?
- Illustrate each creature.

'THE DOOR'

'The Door' is a poem by Miroslav Holub, the Czech scientist and poet – you can find the poem in *The Works: Poems for Key Stage 2* (Macmillan Children's Books, 2006) and Joseph Fiennes performs the poem on *Let's Write Poetry* (BBCACTIV – see Appendices). I don't think that I would begin by reading this aloud to the children – rather, I would hand out copies and ask them to work in small groups to present a reading, thinking carefully about the poem's meaning.

Other activities would include:

- Ask each group to perform the poem in very different ways – using a drum, using chime bars, singing it, slow reading, drum beat after the line 'go and open the door', etc.
- Draw the scene through the door.
- Who is talking to whom?
- How can the darkness tick?
- What is a hollow wind?
- Explain the impact of the last line.
- List words to describe the poem's atmosphere and effect.

Use 'The Door' as a model:

> Go and open the door.
> Maybe there is a sunset dripping over the horizon.
> Maybe there is a tree running away.
> Maybe there is a mole on the ground waiting . . .

You could make the doors more interesting by having them associated with more intriguing concepts, e.g.

> Through the door of disaster,
> I found my mother's wedding ring.
>
> Through the door of eternity,
> I found a shattered mirror.

If they don't want to do doors, then try windows, a gate, a tunnel or a passageway.

Alternatively, you are on an adventure – and have arrived at the end of a corridor. The problem is that you are now faced with lots of doors, each a different colour. What might lie beyond a coloured door?

> Beyond the red door –
> A poppy-faced clown sobs.
>
> Beyond the white door –
> A slice of bread slithers silently
> To the chalky floor.
>
> Beyond the black door –
> Charcoal fingers fumble
> With a cloak made of shadows.

THE OPEN DOOR

Go and open the door of diamonds
you might see a treasure chest
full of metallic medals.

Go and open the door of bones
you might see Cyclops staring back at you.

Go and open the door of wicked claws
you might hear a tiger scratching its prey.

Go and open the door of clocks
you might hear a giant clicking
his fingers in time.

Go and open the door of oysters
you might find a tidal wave
clashing against the mountains.

Go and open the door of computers
you might find a tarantula's website.

Go and open the door of books
you might find
a puzzle of letters.

Go and open the door –
at least the sun will be able to come in.

'THE SICK ROSE'

THE SICK ROSE

O Rose, thou art sick,
The invisible worm
That flies in the night
In the howling storm

> Has found out thy bed
> Of crimson joy,
> And his dark secret love
> Does thy life destroy.
>
> *William Blake*

This is a mysterious poem and there seems to me to be no reason why quite young children shouldn't be presented with a challenge. Once again I would make sure that the children perform the poem – perhaps this time in pairs – using both voices. The poem would also be ideal to set to music and sing as a class.

- Save this poem for the summer – bring in some roses to draw.
- Discuss – how is the rose sick?
- What is the invisible worm?
- What is 'thy bed of crimson joy'?
- Why does 'his dark secret love' destroy the rose's life?
- Talk about what is happening.
- Draw the poem.
- List questions or puzzles for class discussion.

When discussing poems, it is worth explaining the idea of 'being tentative'. Make a list of helpful sentence openers:

> I'm not sure but. . .
> Maybe. . .
> I may be wrong but. . .
> I'm wondering if. . .
> . . . makes me wonder/think. . .
> Perhaps. . .
> Do you think that. . .

'THE VISITOR'

This is a ghost poem by Ian Serraillier. It is ideal for performance. Take time with the children to think through how to perform it – where to vary the pace, use pauses, expression, volume – and what sort of background sound effects might help. It could be performed by a group while several children act the scene out. Other activities:

- Hot seat William and his Wife.
- Why did William take the ring?
- Why did he give it to his wife?
- Whose was it?
- Tell the story of how the ring got lost in the first place.
- Write either William or his wife's diary the next day.
- Paint the scenes.
- Prepare background music.
- Prepare a PowerPoint (or similar) presentation using paintings, music and voices.

'THE LISTENERS'

'The Listeners' is less scary than 'The Visitor'. It is a hard poem to read and may be best tackled in sections by the children to produce a class version for assembly performance.

- Perform the poem.
- Act the poem out.
- Paint the scene.
- Select music to match the poem from a bank of musical clips.
- Read the poem over the top of your chosen music.
- Try reading the poem as a rap.
- Hot seat the traveler.
- Write his diary entry or a letter to a friend.
- Write a message for the traveller to leave.
- Role play a conversation in a tavern between the traveller and a friend.

- Interview the horse!
- List questions and puzzles – discuss tentatively as a class.
- Who has the traveller come to see?
- Is it a ghost story? Vote on this. The children defend their ideas by finding proof from the poem.
- Who is 'them'?
- What might he have been meeting about ('I kept my word')?
- Who or what are the listeners – why didn't they respond?
- Look through the poem to see how the poet creates different effects, e.g. the alliteration in line four.

CHAPTER 6
Writing workshop ideas

A. PLAYING WITH WORDS AND IDEAS

The new framework for literacy identifies the importance of encouraging children to write playfully and inventively – developing original playfulness with language and ideas. Of course, children do this naturally, from making up silly names to playground chants.

List poems are a simple and effective way of helping children develop confidence as writers. They provide a repeating pattern that acts rather like a coat-hanger so that children can focus upon using words effectively and creating new and interesting ideas, e.g.

> I want to write a poem
> made of a ladybird's scarlet wings.
>
> I want to write a poem
> made of crumbs from the last jammy dodger.
>
> I want to write a poem
> made of the sudden screech
> from a car tyre
> shuddering to stop!

It is worth remembering that many poetry forms are not suitable as models for children's own writing. For instance, whilst we may well enjoy reading a Charles Causley ballad, the form is far too demanding for most children. List poems are ideal because the form does not dominate the writing but allows the children to focus upon creating their own ideas. The form should liberate and not constrain.

One of the problems you may find is that some children may just write dull lists that seem to go on for ever! If this is the case, show them how to elaborate and extend a few of their ideas and then ask them to select their favourite lines and improve them in the same way. Let's say that a child has written:

> With my magic eye
> I saw a snake.

Adding in an adjective and then extending the idea by adding on what the snake was doing might improve this:

> With my magic eye
> I saw a silver snake slithering through the grass.

Of course, it would be even better if we knew what sort of snake it was. And perhaps it might be more playful and surprising (less of a dull cliché) if we had the snake doing something impossible:

> With my magic eye
> I saw a silver rattlesnake
> Winning an award at the Oscars!

There is a strong vein of poetry that plays with language and ideas. This would include the fanciful and fun, the surreal and ridiculous. It ranges from playground rhymes to nonsense verse through to Susan, aged 10:

If only I could wrap the world in a blanket
and
send it to sleep.

If only I could take the laughter from a clown
and shove
it in a bag to take to an auction.

If only I could turn the clouds magnetic and
cram them,
into a suitcase full of iron filings.

If only I could set ablaze to the darkness that
huddles
round you and suffocates you while you are asleep.

If only I could persuade golden pear trees to
grow
on the sun, the pears would burst with delight.

If only I could capture the moon so it
would
cry with happiness when I sprinkled it with salt.

If only I could turn all the books into
stars
so they sparkled with delight when I threw them
up into
the blackness of the night.

Susan, 10 yrs

MAGICAL WISHES

Everybody would like to be granted some magical wishes. Most children have already thought about what they will ask for if they are approached by some sort of wizard or powerful being who can release the world and put it at their fingertips. Making lists of magical wishes can be great fun. You could wish to be transformed, or to see, touch or hear amazing things. Keep the ideas impossible and playful:

I wish I were a star,
glittering silently in the soft dark.

I wish I could see
the stone's heart beating.

I wish I could touch
Jack Frost's icy fingertips
With flames of summer.

I wish I could hear
The bee's yellow thoughts as it
Dances towards a clover patch.

MAGICAL CREATIONS

What would you make if you could create anything? This poetry idea came from Adrian Henri's poem 'I want to paint'. Use the following poem as a model for writing:

I WANT TO CREATE

I want to create
an angry ant as it ambles along,
a terrified tarantula tickling a trout,
and a curious computer calling cautiously to the King.

I want to create
silence closing its lips and vowing never to speak again,
the humming bird's wings flickering,
the sea turning over the beach, scraping the pebbles,
and the tired lorries trundling by.

I want to create the touch of
smooth pebbles from the summer beach,
the stickiness of honey on a fingertip,
and the heat from a teaspoon as it stirs my morning tea.

I want to create the secret of
silence trapped in a candle flame's dance,
a hyena's cackle as it paces its deserted lands,
and the *Titanic's* last scream!

I want to create
the coldness of frost as it freckles the window pane,
the sharpness of a saw as it crunches through wood,
and the sadness of a tear as it trickles down a cheek.

I want to create
the Moon's cold gleam and trap it in a box,
the joy of a merry-go-round as it spins like a wheel,
and the force of a rainbow as it dazzles the sky.

BOASTS & LIES WORKSHOP

The poet James Carter sent me this workshop. James says that it originated from an idea by the poet Jackie Wills. Boasts & Lies is loosely based on a thirteenth century Welsh legend poem and provides a great template structure. It encourages children to be highly imaginative and innovative and to really 'think outside of the box'.

Imagine you are an ancient mythic being, older than time itself. Inside your head is the entire universe. You have observed, lived and experienced all of space and time. You know everywhere and everything – all of history – as well as the present and the future. You know everything that has and could have happened. You have visited every nation, world, galaxy. In this poem, the voice of the mythic being is travelling, echoing through the ether.

This workshop greatly benefits from a brainstorm session at the start. Teachers can write out the structure on the board and encourage children to contribute ideas to each line. A good, credible name for the being is important. Encourage the children to invent their own – names with the letters 'k' 'z' and 'q' often have an authentic ring to them. Letters can even be doubled up – e.g. Zoqquiel or Rakkon. The name of the mythical being can then become the title of the poem.

Not all of the lines in the template have to be included, and classes can include their own or even move these lines around. At times children need to be encouraged to be more adventurous in their thinking so a line such as 'I was there when so-and-so scored the winning goal/when team X won the FA cup', which is quite mundane – could become something more adventurous like 'I was there when the pyramids were built/the first Ice Age began to melt.'

The verse that begins 'And once I was a little. . .' encourages children to write a very short cause-and-effect narrative, that could be something along the lines of. . .

And once I was
   a little grain of wheat
      that made the bread
         that fed the Sultan of Atlantis
            in his last meal
               before his city sank
                  to the depths of the ocean

And once I was
   an angel's tear
      that fell to earth
         grew to a stream
            and filled the oceans of the world

Although the opening stanza rhymes, the rest of the piece benefits from being free verse, as rhyme would greatly restrict the concepts and ideas. Ideas for a poem such as this will commonly come during a number of sittings, so children could be asked to do a number of drafts.

BOASTS & LIES TEMPLATE

My name is [K'azakia / Qu'marrion / Za'no]

I am clever,
strong and wise
and these are neither
boasts nor lies

When I say . . .

I am older than [the first breath of time . . .]

I was there when [the Big Bang blew / evolution began / Moses split the waves]

I remember [the first sunset / Stonehenge's first stone]

I taught [Shakespeare to write / Einstein to think / Columbus to sail]

I know why [the Moon was made]
    and why [the white wolves howl]

I know how many [stars fill the darkness / Trojans built the horse]

In my other lives
  I have been . .
    [a Viking
      a Saxon
        a Persian Princess
        a Greek slave]

And once I was a little . . .
that . . .
then . . .
and then. . .

These are neither
boasts nor lies –

My name is . . .

James Carter (www.jamescarterpoet.co.uk) is a poet/guitarist. He visits primary schools all over the UK to give lively performances and workshops with the express intention of motivating children to write. His latest poetry collection is Time-Travelling Underpants *(Macmillan Children's Books).*

TZA' QUARN

I am Tza' Quarn.

I was once a freckle of water
wrinkling the lake's edge
as man took his first step.

I was once
a golden grain of wheat
spilled from a sack
in Egypt's granary.

I was once an angel's tear.

I was once
a scarlet feather
that fell from the wing
of a red-crested cockerel
that crowed at dawn
when the Vikings attacked.

I was once
a wish that fell from the lips
of a child who tugged
a sword buried deep
in a stone of granite
at the sea's edge.

I was once
a smile that creased the face
of a cruel farmer
as he raised his fist to his servant
and threatened his days with pain.

I was once an apple
   that grew on a tree
      in a garden where nightingales sang
         and a princess who picked me
         and idly played catch.

I was once a sandal
   that trod the desert
      on the foot of one who knew no fear
         and rested then by the well
         where the waters of life sprung.

I was once the guns
   that shuddered and shrieked
      and threw shells of disaster onto cities
         of marble where cool fountains played
         and yellow canaries sang.

I was once a glass slipper
   that was left behind
      when the clock struck midnight
         and the Moon floated in the lake
         with a hive of stars.

Yes – I was once the silence
   after the moment
      when the world began.

I neither boast nor lie.
My name is Tza' Quarn.

INVENTING NEW CREATURES

Begin by making a list of favourite animals. Creatures that work well for writing are often those that have some sort of mythological connections, e.g. wolf, owl, eagle, hawk, kestrel, bear, coyote, spider. To make a new creature you have to choose a colour for your animal, e.g. a red wolf.

To make the new creature where would you find – its voice, its coat, its teeth, its eyes, and its claws. . .? Of course, the colour chosen will guide you. So, to make a red wolf, I will need to make a list of all sorts of red things that I might use, e.g. sunset, flames, postboxes, bus, blood, wine, traffic lights. . . Use a simple pattern to create your new creature.

TO MAKE A RED WOLF

Take,
the sunset as it fades on the horizon,
the roar of lava on Mount Etna
for her voice.

Take,
the smoothness of the postbox's coat,
the scarlet from a soldier's tunic
for her coat.

Take,
the grip of a giant's paw,
the sharpness of a spear's tip
for her teeth.

Take,
the flicker of a fire's flame,
the darkness of despair,
for her eyes.

Take,
the curve of the half Moon,
the flare of a rocket rising
for her claws.

TO MAKE AN OGRE

If I was asked to construct an ogre
I would take –

For skin –
the leathery hide of a rhinoceros,
the rough scrape of granite
and the bristles from a witch's broom.

For bones –
the bark of a gnarled oak tree,
chalk from the Seven Sisters
and the tough shell of a diamond.

For the body –
the kick of a ringmaster's whip,
the ship's mast bending in the wind
and the stride of an African elephant.

For the muscles –
the strength of a dragon's jaw,
the punch of a hurricane's blast
and the force as a tsunami strikes.

For the eyes –
the power of Medusa's stare,
coals from the core of the Earth
and the vision of Cyclops.

For the heart –
the beat of Big Ben's pulse,
the ruthless courage of the Minotaur,
and the cruelty of a thousand wars wrapped into one.

DRAGONS – POEMS ON A THEME

An interesting way to create a literacy unit is to build everything around a theme. Dragons are always popular with any age group. A useful addition to this work would be a copy of Nick Toczek's *Dragon Poems* available from Macmillan Children's Books. There are a number of wonderful poems in the book that would be ideal for class performances – such as 'The Dragon Who Ate the School'. This can be performed with simple percussive background and ideally everyone would be wearing dragon masks!

There are also some good dragon stories that would fit into this unit of work too – ranging from the story of St George through to 'Eragon' by Christopher Paolini. This is a wonderful tale about a young boy who finds a dragon's egg and makes friends with Eragon, the dragon that hatches out! It was written when the author was only 16 years old and is the first in a fantasy trilogy.

The children could begin by looking at images of dragons on the IWB. This might lead into writing a report about dragons in general, using a simple framework:

What it is – definition
What it looks like – description
Where it is found – habitat
What it eats – lifestyle
What it does – more interesting facts
Conclusion – final amazing fact

An imaginative approach would be to create a fantasy Dragon World. Start by drawing the map of the world – it can have a distant mountain, dwarf mines, waterfalls, magical pools, lonely towers. . .this will be used by the children to develop their dragon landscape and make it seem real. Next, they create their own 'dragon passports', designing their own pet dragon.

Dragon Passport

Name: Irana

Age: 60 years

Address: Hedge End, Mount Verania

Distinguishing marks: Green scales, red tail and yellow spots

Food: Vegetarian – eats all vegetables and fruit

Abilities: Flies, breathes fire and can mind-read

Supposing the dragon goes missing? The children might then design a 'wanted' poster to try and find their young dragon. This will need to explain what their pet looks like, where it might be found, what to do if you see it and whom to contact:

Missing – one DRAGON!

Missing girl dragon Irana has green scales and a long red tail. She is smaller than a Shetland pony and cannot be missed because she has yellow spots on her back. Irana's claws are silvery but she keeps them sheathed at all times.

Irana is a gentle young dragon and will only breathe fire if cornered. She eats plants and loves fruit and vegetables. You may only see her at dawn and after sunset because she is shy.

Beware of approaching her from behind as this might scare her. If you spot her do not get too close until you have gained her trust. Contact Wizard Holly if you find her.

Reward 50 golden gemstones.   Holly, year 4.

This can now lead into writing a fantasy story about a young dragon that gets lost or is stolen. But what about the poetry element? A simple starting point is to draw a dragon and annotate it with words and images to describe different parts of the dragon. Now make a simple list of parts of the dragon's body – head, eyes, scales, claws, tail, etc. Use this as a basis for a simple poem in which you take each part of the dragon and create a simile, e.g.

> Eragon's head
> Is bigger than a bus.
>
> His eyes shine
> Like scarlet headlamps.
>
> His scales
> Are tougher than diamonds.
>
> His claws curve
> Like crescent Moons.
>
> His jagged tail can knock
> Blocks of flats over
> with one swipe.

It can be fun to invent different types of dragons. These might be from different places or in different colours. For instance, the Greater Merseyside Ridgeback lives down by the docks in Liverpool. Fact files for different dragons could be produced, including illustrations.

Supposing you discovered a clutch of dragon's eggs. What might they contain? This could become a simple, playful list poem, e.g.

DRAGON'S EGGS

The yellow egg contains
The dragon of sand dunes and egg yolks.

The green egg contains
The dragon of forest leaves and emeralds
Stolen from an Egyptian tomb.

The grey egg contains
The mist off a moor
And the fur of a Siberian wolf.

Try to make each idea special so that you do not just say a green egg is like 'grass' – but make the grass unique by saying what sort it is or where it came from, e.g. 'the green egg contains/the grass from Wembley Stadium.'

Everyone knows that dragons like riddles. Decide on the answer to the riddle, e.g. time, clock, night, silence, moon, feather. Then make a list of what you know about the topic – what it is like, what it does, how it is used. Use these ideas to create an 'I am' riddle. Remember to provide clues but do not give too much away. Puns and plays on words can be useful. In this example, the class brainstormed ideas about a feather.

Initial brainstorm of ideas	Riddle
Soft	I am soft as silk.
Used for flying	I have soared high
Birds have them	Above the hills
Tickles	And yet you might touch me.
Fragile	I will tickle you –
Light as a feather	And though I am frail
Powerful flying	And light as a spider's web
	My power will
	Take you to the highest peak.

A simple way to play with rhyme that leads into writing an effective performance poem is to think about what a dragon might say. Try copying this pattern, which I have borrowed from Adrian Mitchell:

WHAT THE DRAGONS SAY

A dragon says: Yes!
A dragon says: No!
A dragon says: Fly away!
A dragon says: Go!

A dragon says: What's the time?
A dragon says: Magic dust!
A dragon says: Beware!
A dragon says: Trust!

A dragon says: Hide the gold!
A dragon says: I am Greed!
A dragon says: Go away!
A dragon says: Let me feed!

To add extra depth to the children's writing, try experimenting with this idea. Make a list of different emotions such as happiness, sadness, jealousy, misery. Each of these becomes like a dragon lurking inside of you. Use the following pattern to write about your own feelings, e.g.

THE DRAGONS INSIDE OF ME

Inside of me is an angry dragon
Who stomps from room to room.

Inside of me is a tired dragon
Who curls up asleep in the corner.

Inside of me is a curious dragon
Who sticks his nose into everyone's business.

Explore the 'dragons' in society, so a 'dragon' becomes a metaphor for unwelcome aspects of life, e.g.

MODERN DRAGONS

The nightmare dragon
Stirs me in my sleep.

The homework dragon
Pesters me to settle down.

The famine dragon
Stalks the deserts
Thin as a chicken bone.

The bully dragon
Is to be feared –
It waits crouching
When you least expect
Its sudden stabbing words.

Four More Dragon Ideas

DRAGON COUNTING RHYME

One old dragon,
Two dark eyes,
Three magic wishes,
Four evil lies.

A DRAGON ALPHABET

Angrily swooping on innocent towns,
Breathing fire on princess's gowns,
Catching cattle in jagged claws,
Deafening villagers with mighty roars.

> **DRAGON COLLECTIVE NOUNS**
>
> A thunder of dragons
> A crush of dragons
> A roar of dragons.

> **WHAT DO DRAGONS LEARN AT SCHOOL?**
>
> How to fly across the sea.
> How to perch upon a tree.
> How to hide a diamond ring.
> How to mend a broken wing.

SECRET BOXES

Human beings are curious. We all like to know what is going on – whether it is in the latest episode of *Neighbours* or on *Big Brother* or in the lives of those close to us. Boxes also attract us. This has spawned many TV games – the latest being *Deal or No Deal*.

Box poems can make an interesting display. You could write your poems on scrolls, tie them with mini pieces of ribbon and place them inside decorated matchboxes. Or – paste poems on to the sides of shoeboxes and pin these to the wall so that they jut out.

Try making mini boxes using a simple mathematical net. The poems can be placed inside the boxes.

How do you write a box poem? You might want to use Kit Wright's famous 'The Magic Box' poem. This can be found in *The Works: Poems for Key Stage 2* (edited by Pie Corbett, Macmillan Children's Books).

In the poem, Kit envisages what might be contained inside a magical box. To build up the poem, brainstorm a list of possible ideas for what might be kept inside the box. Then list ideas for what it might be made of – and what could be done with the box.

If you cannot find the original, Emily's Poem (see below) will give you the idea.

THE MAGIC BOX

I will put in my box –
the mast of a mossy shipwreck,
sunk beneath the Atlantic Ocean,
lungs of a lonely lake,
slowly breathing before death.

I will put in my box –
a tooth of a glimmering star,
shining brightly for universal light,
the dark pupil of a pencil's lead.

I will put in my box –
the first steps towards a thought in a dream,
and the last footprint of a dinosaur,
before extinction.

I will put in my box –
the thirteenth day in a year and the second moon,
a bird with scales and gills
and a fish with a beak and wings!
flying high over snowy topped mountains
and steep waterfalls.

My box is fashioned from mammoth's bony tusks,
with stripes on the lid and a padlock with a code!
Its hinges are the forks of a shark's teeth,
ready to rip off its divine dinner.

> I shall canoe in my box,
> on and on through the Mississippi river,
> then skim to shore on a pebbly beach,
> the ripple of the river. . .
>
> *Emily, year 5*

The poet Trevor Millum often uses the box idea. He wrote to me explaining how he runs the workshop:

This is an idea inspired by Kit Wright's poem 'The Magic Box'. I introduce the idea of a magic box into which anything can be placed no matter how big or small, how real or imaginary. We are going to give this box to someone very special as a present. The children suggest things which might go in the box and I write them on the board or flip chart without making any judgments or decisions. Sometimes they get in a rut: one child suggests a pussy cat, then there's a puppy, then a hamster and so on – so you have to give some guidance now and then. When we have a collection of about a dozen, we try to put some of them into a verse. It depends on the age of the children how much work they do and how much I do. Imagine we've had a hamster, a kitten, a dinosaur, a sunny day, a football, a football field, a goal, a bar of chocolate, a bag of chips, some flowers, a house and a poetry book (that was obviously to please me!). We try to get them to fit a rhythm of about four beats, so 'a bag of chips', or 'a football field' work well. Others can be made to fit – 'a happy hamster', 'a glorious goal' and then we try to put them in the best order and, if possible, squeeze a rhyme in too. Then it becomes a chant that everyone can join in:

> What's in the box
> In the magic box
> In the box
> In the magic box?
>
> There's a glorious goal
> A kitten at play
> A football field

And a sunny day –
In the box, in the magic box,
In the box, in the magic box.

And so on till we've done two or three verses.

This works particularly well if you have a group of very young children who can't be expected to do much (or any) writing.

Trevor can be contacted at: trevor@fernhse.demon.co.uk www.trevormillum.co.uk Trevor's latest books are a comic strip poem collection, Exploding Heads *(available from NATE (National Association for the Teaching of English www.nate.org.uk) and* A Stegosaurus is for Life, *which is available from Hands Up Books (www.handsup.karoo.net or Amazon).*

SECRETS

All poems are a sort of secret. They reveal little bits of ourselves and little bits about the subject. They are like tiny windows on to our private world of imagination. For a quick-fire starter, hand out strips of paper. Everyone pretends they are the subject that they are writing about – an animal for instance. Each person then invents a secret about an animal and pops it into a hat which you pass round. These can be typed up to make a class list or displayed. You could use the line, 'I'll never tell anyone but . . .'

THE KANGAROO'S SECRET

I'll never tell any one but
I have a city tucked into my pouch.

THE OWL'S SECRET

I'll never tell anyone but
My amber eyes were once marbles.

THE FOX'S SECRET

I'll never tell anyone but
I'm a dab hand at dancing the fox trot.

THE DOLPHIN'S SECRET

I'll never tell anyone but
Dolphins spend most of their time telling jokes.
That is why they smile so much!

Another fun idea is to begin inventing secrets that objects might have. For instance, what sort of secrets would a stone know?

THE STONE'S THREE SECRETS

A sparrow stole a crumb.
The wind is trying to blow the leaves away.
I have a spark trapped inside of me.

Hand out small strips of paper and everyone has to write a magical secret on to the paper. These are then put into a hat and everyone chooses a secret that someone else will have written. Magical secrets are just invented ideas. For instance, here is a list of magical secrets based on the Moon.

THE MOON'S MAGICAL SECRETS

The stars are made of glass eyes.
The night is really just a velvet blanket.
When it is daytime, the moon sleeps.

Move on to something more adventurous by creating a secret.

THE SECRET POEM

My secret is made form –
the fingertips of clouds,
the silence between heartbeats
trapped in a hospital,
the hangman's gloves,
the stoat's bright eye,
the bullet as it slices
through the wind
like the hot knife
slipping through butter.

I found it –
on the edge of a lemon's bite,
clutched in the centre of a crocus,
held in a crisp packet,
crumpled at the side of the road
where the nettle's stab
their sharp barbs
at the innocent child's
soft, eager hand.

This secret can –
prise open hearts made of steel,
smooth a stormy sea flat
capture the wind,
sip the Moon's shine
in an empty palm,
break apart Mount Everest
till it is powder
in a locket.

If I lost this secret –
even the lonely goat left at the roadside
would bleat.

This can act as a model. The pattern is quite simple.

- What is the poem made of?
- Where was it found?
- What can it do?
- What happens if it gets lost?

Create a class version and brainstorm a range of ideas for each section. Below is an example by Eleanor (year 5) that might also be shared with the children.

MY SECRET

My secret is made of –
the steady beat of an Indian's drum,
and a deer's strong horn,
the velvet of a peach's skin,
and a past that has faded,
a panther's teeth like chopping knives,
and the end of a ruined world.

I found my secret –
dancing in the shadows by an abandoned railway,
riding a wild bull across the endless plains,
in a forgotten box in the creaking attic,
waiting to be freed,
within an Impressionist's painting at the London gallery,
and at the tip of the vorpal blade.

This secret can –
break out from Wormwood Scrubs,
make a new moon full,
decide the future for the human race,
climb a rainbow,
then with break-neck speed,
roller coast down the opposite side.

You see, if I lost my secret,
even the soldiers in the Second World War would pause . . .

B. OBSERVATION AND EXPERIENCE

Years ago I used to have two big signs in my classroom. The first read, 'Are you an Observer?' Learning to look carefully lies at the heart of good writing. Noticing the details can help to bring poetry and narrative alive. Most children need to be trained to look carefully and respond with all the senses to experiences. This idea lies at the heart of the poetry progression in the new framework for literacy – the detailed recreation of closely observed experience.

Of course, we write best about what we know and what matters to us. This is the difference between telling children that they are going to write about a pet and bringing into the classroom a tarantula in a perspex cage! The real thing generates interest and means that if we look carefully then we can see what it actually is like.

The other notice read, 'Are you a word-searcher?' Being interested in words and searching for the right one also lies at the heart of effective writing. If you are not a word-searcher then your writing will be lazy, bland and clichéd. Finding the right word to illuminate the truth of an experience means pausing, generating possibilities and then selecting the right word. This is developed by lots of class brainstorms.

It is worth spending time seeking out objects, pieces of art or images that can be used as starting points for writing. Here is a list of possibilities:

- **observing an experience** – leaf skeletons, a spider's web, a pomegranate sliced in half
- **objects/collections** – tree bark, hands, candles, buttons, ties, photos, feathers
- **locations** – old buildings, woods, alleyway, sea front, building site
- **unusual objects** – back of a broken TV set, a ship-in-a-bottle

- **art** – drawing before writing, postcards/posters of paintings, music, sculptures, film clips, photos, dance
- **seasons and weather** – thunder, storms, rain, snow, frost, dew
- **relationships** – things mum says, my teacher is. . ., friends, enemies
- **memories** – secret places, details, strange events, old dreams, things I used to do
- **feelings** – anger, sadness, elation, memorable incidents
- **a recalled common experience** – bonfire night, dark in my room

Weaker writers need to have the focus for writing in front of them. This means bringing something into the classroom or taking the children outside so that they can see something. The teacher then draws the children's attention to different aspects of the focus and the children start brainstorming ideas. These can be captured on a board – listing words, images, and phrases. This will, later on, act as a resource bank for less confident writers. More importantly, the teacher is training the children to observe and generate words and ideas rapidly.

SENSES LIST POEM

Begin by writing simple list poems based on the senses:

I want to listen to the sound of cars racing.
I want to listen to the sound of the TV rumbling downstairs
    while I am trying to sleep.

Then demonstrate how to write a 'crazy senses' poem, mixing the senses up, e.g.

I want to touch the scent of sunlight shimmering.
I want to touch the sound of the whale's last echo.
I want to touch a baby's first cry and the sadness of the final
    gasp, etc.

At first, demonstrate and then start taking the children's ideas – scribing in front of the children on a flip chart. Encourage interesting ideas and push the children to select words and ideas with care. Establish the notion that 'first thought is not always the best thought' – keep sifting and fishing for ideas and then select the most powerful.

Then let the children write their own list poem using their own ideas. The point of this activity is to alert the children to using their senses and to begin to develop the ability to choose powerful language and interesting combinations rather than clichés.

THE THINGS AROUND YOU

Raymond Carver advised writers to 'make use of the things around you'. This is good advice. Writers have to get good at making something of their experience, noticing what would make good 'copy'. I'm writing this on a train to Leicester, the second to last day of the Christmas term. So let me make use of what is around me to create a little snapshot for you, so you too can see what I can see and hear. In that way my poem becomes a little word machine that will let you see and experience in your imagination something vaguely like what I am seeing.

> Make use of the things around you –
> The man sitting opposite me
> On the 5.15 to Leicester
> sips his tea.
> His stryofoam cup sweats.
> The Twix bar glitters false bronze.
> Water bubbles in my water rise and pop.
> The tap of computers by commuters.
> The low hum of conversation.
> A mum leans forwards to chat to her daughter.
> Reflections in the train window are mirror images.

> Beyond, the darkness slides by.
> Town lights glitter.
> Road lights are like bright orange necklaces.
> Wellingborough station is a dark shadow.
> Passengers pace, restless with the cold.

This sort of looking and listing could easily be done anywhere. Philip Gross asks students to look for something in the room – something small and insignificant that no-one else has noticed – as a starting point. In a classroom we might list the following things to use:

> The paint peeling like a scab,
> The computer's blank face,
> The pencil shavings curled into spirals
> Like miniature carpets,
> The God's Eyes staring down at us,
> The row of dictionaries packed
> With a million words.

The secret is to make each thing that you look at a little special by using words in a slightly unexpected fashion.

CANDLES

Candles never fail to produce good writing. There is something mesmeric about the experience that always captures the imagination. So begin by darkening the room as best as possible. Light the candle and then begin the brainstorm. Draw the children's attention to the flame, how it moves, the wax, the candle itself. End by blowing it out. To generate similes, it can help to draw a flame shape and ask the children what it looks like or reminds them of – a leaf, an eye, a spear. . .

Draw a simple candle shape on a board and then use some of the words gathered to create a simple shape poem.

The
flame
flickers
restlessly
dodging
and darting
like an amber
eye peering
out of the
darkness.

HANDS

Begin this lesson by demonstrating on a board how to draw
your hand. Encourage the children to look closely and
carefully – if you have magnifying glasses these can help, as
the children will see more clearly the lumps and bumps that
create what can look more like a lunar landscape than simple
skin.

Now brainstorm words and list them. Keep this very rapid so
that you encourage excitement and rapid thinking. Get them
to look at the back of their hands, knuckles, fingernails and
tips, palms, fingerprints, lines across their hands. What are
they like? What do they remind you of?

Now use a few of the ideas listed and write a short class poem
together in simple free verse – some short lines and some
longer. Remember to use some technique – choosing 'good'
words, a touch of alliteration and some similes, e.g.

> My hand is like a five-fingered crab.
> The knuckles tighten,
> like white ridges.
> My palm is a map of roads
> that carries my destiny.
> My fingernails are jagged moons,
> ready to scratch and scrape.

THISTLE IN THE PLAYGROUND

The more you introduce children to the range of poetic possibilities, the more they have to call upon. Take a walk round the playground. What is unusual or striking? Choose a subject and then draw on the list of possibilities. For instance, you could:

- Make comparisons
- Talk to it
- Reveal secrets
- Tell lies
- Pretend
- Describe it
- Bring it alive
- Ask questions
- Boss it around
- Make a list about it
- See it from different angles
- Personify it
- Use surprising combinations
- Make a riddle
- Boast about it
- Exaggerate
- Make it talk – monologue
- Word play
- Capture it in a word snapshot

Last time I tried this, I was in London. I had noticed a thistle growing up through the tarmac at the edge of the playground. We sat round looking. I had brought out the flip chart so we could try out some ideas. I started by asking what it reminded them of – what it looked like – what it was doing. We ended up with:

> The thistle leans
> To one side,
> Bristling with sharp points
> And snake's tongues.
>
> The thistle is a crown of thorns
> Ready to stab your leg.
>
> It punched its way,
> Restlessly, through the tarmac
> Reaching up to the light.
>
> Out of the darkness
> It burst;
> Out of the cold
> It rose;
> Out of the earth
> It sprang.
>
> Where did it find such determination?
> Where did it steal such green?
>
> This thistle is the last
> Grassy fist of King Arthur,
> It is the last tooth of anger,
> The final sword.
>
> It's secrets will be scattered on the wind.

Try choosing a subject that everyone can see and then draw on the possibilities that you have discovered through reading other poems that you have worked on as well as poetry warm-ups and writing workshops.

Writing workshop ideas

WEATHER – SNOW AND STORMS

The weather is a powerful force in children's lives. Snow and storms provide a common experience that both fascinates and resonates as a subject for writing. Ideally, the day after a thunderous night or a first fall of snow should be seized. Other plans abandoned, the wise teacher knows that when children are interested, they are motivated – and they learn best and write best when motivated.

Choose a specific focus, e.g. snow fall. Brainstorm with the class as many words as possible to provide a massive bank of words. It can help if you collect words in bunches so the brainstorm is vaguely organized. If you were brainstorming you might organize it like this:

Thunder sounds – *rumble, grumble, moan, groan, bang, boom . . .*
What thunder sounds like – *a giant, saucepans, an argument, gunfire, drum beats, cannons, explosions, bombs . . .*
Lightning colours – *white, silver, purple*
What lightning looks like – *pattern, puzzle, broken vase, rip, tear, jagged tin, map lines, roads, veins . . .*
How lightning strikes – *hit, slide, slither, slip, crash, smack, crack, crackle, whip, lash, shatter, splinter . . .*
How rain falls – *wash, run, hisses, spits, splashes, strikes, shivers, shimmers, quivers, rivers, spills, taps, beats . . .*
Looking from the window I see/hear – *leaves tumble, newspaper roll, trees bend, telegraph lines bow, streets glisten, rain glitters . . .*

You will notice that the words collected are ones that bring the experience alive – that help the writer to recreate – they show what happens rather than telling the reader.

If they are experienced, they can move straight into writing, though you may wish to set them off by reading a few examples of good writing saved from a previous year. Here are a couple to get you going:

131

ICY BREATH

The wind crashes
With a piercing squeal
Into the arched reeds
Ripping the green
To pieces of thread.
Hair bellows out
As the wind cuts
Into your face.
Fiercely,
It bends saplings.
Shredding leaves,
Throwing fragments
Into the air.

Tim, 9 yrs.

STORM

The thunder
Splits silence, shatters calm.
Sky rent,
Wrenched into a muscular
Explosion. Lightning
Spears, veins slender and
Slim spitting
Acute to the ground.
Forked yellowy
Threads spill, zig-zagging
To Earth.
Rain rages in fury,
Beating, driving,
Its icy whips to
The window
Panes, cascading down
In streams
Of punches, ricocheting off
car boots.

Ramon, 10 yrs.

You will notice that Ramon uses a simple pattern (broken only once). I had asked the children to use a word count pattern to shape their writing.

Once children know how to look, generate words and ideas, the teacher just has to find interesting experiences for the children. Here are few close observation poems:

SNOW

It grips on roofs.
It camouflages trees, it makes a quick disguise.
The snow covers the world like a massive sheet.
The wind bitterly bites into your flesh, it
Tosses the snow all around the town.
Icicles form on the roof edges and window
Panes, someone breaks one and it shatters into
Tiny fragments, it splinters.
Suddenly a blaze of sunlight sheets through
The clouds.

Julian, 9 yrs.

SUGAR

His luminous eyes glint
In the darkness
Of the evening.
His sleek slender tail sways
In the bitter breeze.
He winks lovingly at me.
He arches his back
And kneads
On the dew wet grass,
His mouth strains open,
His jagged teeth
Embedded in his jaw.
The roof of his mouth
Is crinkled.
You can see his cold
Elegant bones
Arching his jaw.

Richard, 9 yrs

MY HOBBY

I sit concentrating,
Silent.
My float droops.
The air stops breathing.
The current slows.
Tense,
I tighten every muscle,
Taut as the finest wire.
My rod bends
At fifty degrees.
It whips back
To zero.
The water swallows my float.
The trace glides down.
My nylon snapped!

Tim, 10 yrs

SITTING IN THE BATH

Silent, steaming.
Condensation slithers stealthily
From the shimmering mirror
Of water.
Echoes blink.
Ripples ricochet on the bath.
I hesitate
As I dip my elbow in.
Whirling the cold water,
I clamber in.

Ramon, 9 yrs

GOODBYE

Silky fur grey with age
Crystal eyes look lovingly
Black ears droop tiredly
Stumpy tail unable to say
Goodbye.

Thomas, 7 yrs

WRITING 'ON LOCATION', e.g. AT THE FARM

Writing on location depends on the weather. While on location demonstrate to the children how to look carefully at the details of a focus – and jot down words, ideas, similes, using the senses.

Select one thing that makes a powerful focus and, as a group, brainstorm – draw their attention to detail and using the senses. Ask them 'What does it look like? What does it remind you of?'. When looking at something, it can help to jot down the main things that you can see down the centre of the page – tongue, jaws, teeth, saliva, flanks, hooves. Then add words either side of each thing – adjectives / verbs, etc.

horns

Then add in words:

Curved horns nod

It is also worth having a 'What does it look like' column for similes:

Curved horns nod twin scimitars

Then, on a flip chart show them how to take the brainstorm ideas and craft them into a simple, descriptive free-verse poem, e.g.

The cow snorts and snuffles,
rubbing her heaving flanks against the railing.
Her horns jut out of her skull
like a Viking helmet,
like handle bars on a lunar monster.
Eyes bulge,
staring like glassy marbles.
Spittle drips from her jaws
as she grinds her teeth,
chewing over
the passing day.

Demonstrate how to select details and then make more of them, e.g.

Horns
Eyes
Spittle
Teeth

Show how each word can be added to, e.g.

Grey **horns** jut up.
Wild **eyes** glare like frozen glass.
A string of **spittle** dangles down.
Her **teeth** grind together
like tiny millstones.

Add powerful language and use a dash of poetic technique.

SNAPSHOTS

Haiku is a traditional form of Japanese poetry – where it has three lines and uses a pattern of 5, 7, 5 syllables. Over-focusing on the number of syllables may spoil a good poem so it is often best to encourage the children to write a short poem without the constraints of syllable counting. Haiku reflect a season, and build a mini snapshot of a moment in time. The idea is to express a feeling or idea through the concrete description of 'things'. One simple technique is to organize the haiku in the following way:

Line 1: season and time of day: *Early winter morning.*
Line 2: something you can hear: *Frost crackles underfoot.*
Line 3: something you can see: *Cars slalom down the lane.*

I have found that using the interactive whiteboard to show pictures of seasons is a helpful stimulus.

Tanka traditionally use five lines, adding two extra lines on to a haiku each of seven syllables.

> Heat haze, horizon burns.
> Fields of corn send scorching flames,
> Leaping high skywards.
> Smoke drifts over chalk-backed hills.
> Sunburnt walkers stalk homewards.
>
> *Mike, 12 yrs*

Cinquain were invented by an American writer with the memorable name of Adelaide Crapsey. There are five lines with a syllable pattern of 2, 4, 6, 8 and 2. The final line is usually a comment or surprise. This creates an interesting shape on the page. An easier version of the cinquain uses a word count of 1, 2, 3, 4, 1 words per line, e.g.

GRAVE CINQUIAN

Tidied
kingdoms and
simple tell-tale mounds
that privileged rails keep
apart.

Stuart, 15 yrs

A kenning is an old English and Norse form, which is a type of riddle, where the subject is renamed. So a sword becomes 'flesh-biter' or the sea is a 'whale-road'. You could bring in a collection of objects as starting points for writing kennings, e.g. a mirror, a key, a clock, a banana, a bottle, a pair of glasses and so forth. It can be helpful to make a list of possible well-known creatures, e.g. dog, cat, monkey, crocodile, elephant etc.

Choose one item to use as a whole-class example – let's say the glasses. Now brainstorm everything that the class can think about glasses, e.g. helps you see, made of glass, sit on nose, attached to ears, look through, sun reflects off them, can get sunglasses, can't see without them, teachers peer through them . . .

Now take an idea and show how to begin to turn this into the kenning form, e.g.

Nose percher
Ear hugger
World viewer
Sight clearer

Twin windows
Sun defeater
Blind chaser
Sight reflector

Ezra Pound's poem 'In a Station of the Metro' is a simple comparison poem. In his poem the first line states what he can see – the faces of people coming out of the underground. In the second line, he compares them to the petals of a lily on a black bough.

This simple format makes a useful pattern for exploring comparisons. First of all select some sort of striking scene or object that can be seen and seems to resonate, e.g.

A thorn sticks out from the bramble

Now think of what the thorn looks like and generate a simile, e.g. *like a bull's horn.*

Extend the image so that is even more like the first line, e.g. *like a bull's curved horn, waiting.*

Now get rid of the word 'like' and bring the two lines together using a semi-colon, e.g.

> A thorn sticks out from the bramble;
> a bull's curved horn, waiting.

BRINGING THE WORLD TO LIFE

One of the extraordinary things that a poem can do is to bring the world to life – making it sound as if objects could move or animals speak. A poem like Blake's 'The Tyger' (found in *The Works: Poems for Key Stage 2*) is an interesting example of someone talking to an animal or inanimate object. This might easily lead into writing poems in which we talk to other animals or ask questions. For instance, we might talk to a wolf:

Wolf –
where did you find your misty fur
and your eyes that pierce the night?

Wolf –
why do you lope along so silently,
avoiding man's company?

Wolf –
have you just crept out of a child's tale
or are you really out there waiting, waiting?

Of course, animals or objects might speak back. Poets can adopt the role of a creature, an object, a mood or a season and speak for themselves.

I am the night.
I smother the world
half by half
in a cloak of darkness.
I am silent –
and leave as soon
as daylight appears.

To encourage children to bring the world to life, it can be helpful to introduce them to the idea of personification. Personification is a technique that treats inanimate objects as if they were alive. To introduce the idea, make a simple list of things that humans do – stare, jump, cry, giggle, dream, snore, climb trees. Then make a list of objects that can be seen in the room – window, chair, table, pencil, door, clock, book. Now put the lists together to bring the room to life:

The window stares,
the chair jumps,
the table cries,
the pencil giggles,
the door dreams,
the clock snores,
and the book climbs trees.

It doesn't take much to add in a few adjectives and extend some of the lines to create a lively and imaginative scene:

> The glassy-eyed window stares out at the world,
> While the wooden chairs jump for joy,
> And the old table cries mournful, wooden tears.
> The pencil pot giggles to itself,
> while the door daydreams of winning at Wimbledon.
> As the weary clock snores,
> the books run outside to climb trees.

You can use the same sort of technique to write about scenes, faces, images and paintings. The following poem is based on a photo of London at night – any picture will do, just apply the same technique. This is how I wrote the poem.

First of all, I looked at the picture. I made a list of the six main things that I could see in the picture and wrote them down the centre of a blank page like this:

lights

cars

buses

buildings

pavements

doorways

I then took each idea in turn and used personification – bringing it alive as though my ideas were creatures:

lights glare

cars snarl

buses busy themselves

buildings straighten

pavements snake

doorways yawn

I then decided that I would add in some adjectives, using alliteration and extending some of the ideas:

> Late night city lights glare,
> glowering on street corners.
>
> Cruising cars snarl by,
> their drivers wearing ghostly masks.
>
> Buses busy themselves
> at street corners,
> greeting customers
> with sudden warmth.
>
> Buildings straighten
> to attention like
> dark giants high above.
>
> Far below, pavements snake
> across the city
> like lines on the palm
> of a map's hand.
>
> Doorways yawn.
> Dawn is a cup of coffee away.

MEMORY POEMS

Play games based on memory searches. List great holidays, times spent with old relatives, birthdays, special occasions, sad times, funny times, memorable moments, times I was in trouble – all this can begin to provide a bank of anecdotes that might become sources for poems later on.

- Excuses for being late or not doing homework;
- When my best friend left school, I remember. . .
- When I started at school – my first day. . .
- When I was in the infants . . .
- My first school friend . . .
- Two minute burst writing about a memory. . .
- Scabs – what happened that left you with that mark!

MEMORIES OF THE PLACE

Visits to local places can be used to generate imaginative writing. Suppose these walls could speak. What memories does this house contain?

- Use names of previous inhabitants or invent names of people who might have worked there.
- Use simple lists to aid writing, e.g.
  - Long ago I heard. . . /Long ago I saw. . .
  - In role as a mirror: Once I saw. . .
  - This room recalls . . .
  - This room once heard/saw. . .
  - This house has seen/heard . . .
  - If these walls could speak they would tell you about. . .

Here is an example about my own house:

This room once heard
A parrot twittering to itself
Like a fussy old lady,
Preening her feathers.

This room once saw
Tea cakes and bone china,
Waiting nervously
For Mother to pour
For her poor son
Back from the War.

This room once saw
A baby crying, its face
Screwed tight as an angel's fist
And howling in rage.

This room once tasted
The scent of roses,
Red as blood
And fresh from a garden
Down the lane,
Stolen for a loved one.

This room remembers
A boy curled tight
On his bed
Reading *The Beano*
beneath the sheets,
with a torch gripped
between his teeth
and the tent of sheets glowing.

MEMORIES OF IMAGES OR OBJECTS

This can be quite a quick-fire game. Each child selects or is given an object or image, or you make a list of possible subjects, e.g. *lake, raindrop, key, window, door, window, tree, hand, ring, clock,* etc.

The children are timed and only have, say, two minutes (depending on their writing speed) and have to write down what the object remembers. Supposing a stone could remember. Here is an idea:

The tree's first memory

I remember bursting through the soil and seeing the Sun for the first time. I remember my bark thickening as it stretched up higher and higher. I remember the first shock of autumn as my leaves withered.

The raindrop's first memory

As I left the comfort of the cloud, I fell a thousand feet until I hit a window pane. I remember dribbling down the pane and watching the television inside.

You could use a simpler frame, e.g.

I remember seeing. . .
I remember hearing. . .
I was witness to. . . .

MEMORY BOXES

Children bring in a memory box – containing photos or objects that all hold a memory. It is worth getting them to show what they have brought and tell the 'memory'. Demonstrate how to write a simple free-verse poem based on a memory, e.g.

When I was eight,
I got lost at the zoo –
I remember stumbling
Like an alien
Amongst adults
Vast as sailing ships
Whilst I was the little dinghy adrift
In an uncharted sea.

They may need to 'tell the experience' on to the page rather like an anecdote – and then begin shaving it back, using some technique to hone its poignancy. It can help to get them to read their writing aloud and to listen for the parts that flow like free verse and which bits descend into prosey storytelling.

SIX WAYS OF LOOKING

This idea came from a poem by the American writer Wallace Stevens who wrote a poem called 'Thirteen Ways of Looking at a Blackbird'. In each mini verse, Stevens views the Blackbird in a different manner. I have simplified the idea and found that it can lead to some very intriguing mini poems. Each child chooses a focus for writing. This could be anything from an animal to something dull like a gate or an ironing board. Now make a list of possible focuses for each section of their poem. For instance, one line might have to use alliteration – another might have to use a simile:

Poetry instructions	Model poem
	8 ways of looking at a loaf of bread
1. A simile using 'like'	1. The slices are like a deck of cards.
2. An instruction	2. Get into the toaster and do not burn!
3. A question	3. Bread, why do you keep loafing about?
4. A wish	4. The loaf wishes that the knife would stop looking her way!
5. A lie	5. Bread swims.
6. Personification and alliteration	6. The bold bread lay on the brassy beach and put on its sunglasses.

The following poem came as a result of working through a few sample poems as a class on the board. I made a list of possible subjects for the children to select from: lake, river, key, lock, tower, forest, flame, Moon, sun, eye, stars, map, leaf, tree, snake, etc. On this occasion everyone chose a different topic. I just asked them to make a list in which they approached the subject differently.

SIX WAYS OF LOOKING AT A POND

1. A pond's ripple shatters faces into misery and lines.
2. A pond reflects the memories of children playing by its edge.
3. Sheets and sheets of lace, gently laid on top of each other, glistening in the sunlight.
4. A pond is a net of faces and fish being dragged behind a trawler.
5. A pond is a glittering pocket of beads trickling into a bag.
6. A pond is a swan's paradise, where she gazes into the darkness.

Kathryn, 10 yrs

The following poem came as a result of looking at poems about cats by George MacBeth. He has one poem titled '14 Ways of Touching the Peter'. The poem has 14 short verses, each of seven lines, using 14 words. We brainstormed words that we could use instead of touch – stroke, nudge, hold, tickle, squash, rub, etc.

Then we invented verses together. Jamie managed 14 words in nearly all his verses – but as the children were so young, I allowed some leeway!

SIX WAYS TO TOUCH LUCKY

You can stroke his
Jet black fur while
He purrs and prowls
Nudging you.

You can tickle him
Under his chin until
He arches his back
Into a bridge.

You can squash his
Warm soft back as
He rests next to the
Fire.

You can rub his
Furry tail until
He scratches you
And cuts your
Hands.

You can feel his soft
Fat tummy
And his heart
Beating very fast.

Jamie, 8 Years

Another strategy is to issue instructions and give the children one or two minutes to write each line. This poem is an example that came from a year 4 class. I set the game up as a challenge. I gave an instruction and the children had a minute or two to write the line. Then we moved on to the next. At the end, I gave five minutes for re-reading and polishing. We listed possible openings, e.g. this morning, this evening, at night, in the midnight hour, at dawn, last night, etc. Here is Tim's poem alongside my instructions. It took about 15 minutes from start to finish.

Instructions	Pupil's example
• How did you come to school – by what unusual method?	This morning I came to school on a bone-dry tongue.
• Something happens to an object in this room.	This morning a book cracked open and the words fell out.
• Include a number or letter.	This morning number 5 was seen by a hive.
• Include a colour.	This morning the colour red was dreaming upside down in his bed.
• Include a character from a book.	This morning C.S. Lewis knocked on my door to see Aslan.
• Include an animal.	This morning a baboon popped a balloon.
• What happened to an abstract idea – sorrow, hope, fear, hatred, etc.	This morning sorrow giggled.
• Include the past or future.	This morning the past came as a flame and I wrung its neck.
• End with a contrast.	In the evening I called the morning to me and sliced it to shreds.

WRITING POEMS USING ALPHABETS, DAYS AND MONTHS

'Solomon Grundy' is an old rhyme that was first written down in 1842. You can use the pattern of something happening on different days of the week for all sorts of possibilities. For instance, you could write a list of what different people do. . . with a twist, e.g.

On Monday, the banker
burned all the money.

On Tuesday, the builder
began to use soap instead of bricks.

On Wednesday, the hairdresser
swapped her scissors for a lawnmower. . .

To write a calendar poem, like Christina Rossetti, is a little harder. I began by listing the months and trying to think of something that happens during that month, e.g. mad March hares! Or, April Fools' day. Then I wrote my poem, trying to make each idea different.

There are many ways to use alphabets. You could use people's names and make each line alliterate, e.g.

Amy ate an awful apple.
Boris built a bold banana.
Candy carefully caught a cautious crab. . .

You could also try writing an alphabet poem that uses place names and states what happens there (an atlas or map helps), e.g.

In Andover
they sit in clover.

In Battle
they rattle.

In Cheam
they dream.

In Dundee
they eat tea. . . .

SOLOMON GRUNDY

Solomon Grundy
Born on a Monday
Christened on Tuesday,
Married on Wednesday,
Took ill on Thursday,
Worse on Friday,
Died on Saturday,
Buried on Sunday.
That was the end of
Solomon Grundy.
Traditional

THE CAT BURGLAR'S WEEK

On Monday, I could smell fish
and found scales in the bathroom.

On Tuesday, I followed paw prints
but they were an impoverished read.

On Wednesday, I saw a tail,
the end waving goodbye to me.

On Thursday, I bought some perfume
and all afternoon was irritated by
by the sound of soft murmurings.

On Friday, I took a nap
and, for some reason, felt lonely.

On Saturday, I opened a bag
but there was nothing inside.

And on Sunday, I realised that somebody
had nabbed the cat.

THE MONTHS

January, cold and desolate;
February dripping wet;
March wind ranges;
April changes;
Birds sing in tune
To flowers of May,
And sunny June brings longest
    day;
In scorched July
The storm clouds fly,
Lightning-torn;
August bears corn,
September fruit;
In rough October
Earth must disrobe her;
Stars fall and shoot
In keen November;
And night is long
And cold is strong
In bleak December.

Christina Rossetti

CALENDAR POEM

January, snow falls
disguising the streets.
In February, the Moon sulks.
March, and the crazy hare
Lip-reads the wind.
April begins with a fib.
It's May, and flower petals
explode in the park.
June, the sun
flexes its muscles.
July, the clouds tussle.
August, ice cream vans
blossom on beaches.
September, reaches for a coat.
October, the cold
sneaks upstairs.
November, a bonfire flares,
blooming in the backyard.
December, mince pies
are mugged by the stars.

AN ANIMAL POEM BY NUMBERS

One is the whale that sat still as a fist.
Two is the mouse that got kissed in the mist.

Three is the python that decided to dance.
Four is the cheetah that sailed off to France.

Five is the hippo that hoped for honey.
Six is the snake that saved all his money.

Seven is the slug that wanted to cook.
Eight is the worm that ate the whole book.

Nine is the newt that needed a nappy.
Ten is the croc that was far too snappy.

A NECKLACE POEM BY NUMBERS

One is a sun blazing.
Two is a freckle on a robin's speckled egg.
Three is the centre of a sunflower.
Four is the sound of a church bell echoing.
Five is a crop circle that appeared overnight.
Six is a golden plate in a dragon's hoard.
Eight is a lie that has a familiar ring to it.
Nine is a nettle rash.
Ten is the end of a cuckoo's call.
Eleven is the space where the master lays his head
in the lion's mouth.
Twelve is a pancake that tastes of lemon.
Thirteen is ok.
Fourteen is the burning eye of Blake's tyger.
Fifteen is a rosebud before it bursts open.
Sixteen is a cold marble stuck under a chair.
Seventeen is a fist, raised for peace.
Eighteen is the first apple that grew in the garden.
Nineteen is the football that scored the winning goal.
Twenty is the Moon's reflection, never caught in a lake.

How I wrote my two Poems by Numbers

I have always liked Charles Causley's poetry. His poem 'A Poem by Numbers' seemed to me to be a clever idea because it used a simple pattern but also told a story. I noticed that the lines could be read individually or as a sequence.

I decided to have a go at writing my own version. First of all, I thought that I would try and make the poem rhyme. I decided to make it easy for myself so I thought that I would write a list of animals in a zoo that were all doing crazy things.

'An Animal Poem by Numbers' is written in couplets, using rhyme. This was not too difficult. To start, I made up the first line of each couplet. Then I made a list of possible rhyming words to help me invent the second line. Some of the first lines I had to change, as I couldn't find a sensible rhyme. I used *Black's Rhyming and Spelling Dictionary* to help.

To get the rhythm, I kept saying the lines aloud and listened to them. The pattern of each line had to imitate its neighbour. Tapping out the beat of the line can help but I find that saying it aloud is vital. You may need to shorten or lengthen a line to get the same rhythm for each pair.

Having written 'An Animal Poem by Numbers', I decided to try something serious. I got the idea from an old string of beads that my grandmother gave me. The beads came from Kenya and each bead is carved into a different shape. I wondered what each bead – each sphere – reminded me of, and I made a list of round things – sun, egg, plate, apple, football, porthole, ring, wheel, eyeball, orange, beachball, cooking ring, bottom of a glass, glasses, letter O, a seed, a nail's head and so on.

I began writing my first line, 'One is a sun blazing'. This seemed rather ordinary so after that I tried to make each idea special. For instance, my second line was going to be, 'Two is an egg'. To make it special, I decided that it would be a robin's egg, then I thought that it might be a speckled robin's egg. Next, I added in the idea that 'two' might be the freckle on a speckled robin's egg.

THE SIX SIDES OF A DICE

The first side shows
A small black hole
On a large patch of snow.

The second side shows
Twins standing silently
Side by side.

The third side shows
The winning line
A game of noughts and crosses.

The fourth side shows
Corner of a boxing ring
Before the fight begins.

The fifth side shows
Four subjects
Bowing before their king.

The sixth side shows
Soldiers
Guarding the Queen's palace.

Sally, 10 years

CHAPTER 7
Shakespeare rules

THE METAPHORICAL MOUSE

Words are metaphors – they represent something. They claim to be what they are not. You say the word 'stone' and that becomes a stone – but it is not. It is just a sound. The metaphor helps a writer make an idea visible. The writer doesn't just liken one thing to another but one thing becomes another; the identity of one thing is imprinted upon another. Methaphors are more powerful than similes. With simile, the reader is made aware of the device so it may well sound forced. Metaphor is more subtle because the reader may not be aware of its use. But metaphor presupposes a simile. The metaphor grows out of a likeness, but it is more economical.

For an image to work well it must be shocking and appropriate. Shocking in that it makes the reader pause, stunned for a second by something new and revelatory. Appropriate because it must be true and telling. A well crafted image surprises the reader by helping us see the world anew. The image helps us imagine and takes us to the core of both what the writer felt and the experience itself. It is the freshness of vision, or word combination, that works, rather than the child recycling a dead metaphor or simile that has been used a million times before and therefore brings nothing new.

SHAKESPEARE RULES

One cold summer's evening, we were watching an outdoor production of *A Midsummer Night's Dream* when I noticed the lines:

> I must go seek some dew-drops here
> And hang a pearl in every cowslip's ear
>
> (Act 2, Sc. 1: 14–15)

I began wondering what other tasks a fairy or imp might have to accomplish. While the play was continuing, I began to note down some ideas:

> There is so much to do –
> I must sprinkle flecks of frost
> On the crisp autumn leaves.
> I must seize the hiss of an adder
> And hang dew on a spider's web.
> I must help the blind mole
> Build pyramids of earth.
> I must sharpen blades of grass
> And put freckles on a child's face.
> I must howl with the gale
> And dance with the March hare
> On the whale-backed hillside.
> I must catch the silvery light
> That slips from the Moon's white face.
> I must push green shoots
> Through the stubborn earth
> And ride on the bumblebee's back.
> I must polish the salmon's scales
> Till they shine like sunlight.
> I must tip dreams into the lover's ear
> So he can hear his wishes.

Using lines from Shakespeare or any other great writer can often act as a way into internalizing memorable language as well as acting as a catalyst for children's creativity. For instance:

In nature's infinite book of secrecy
A little I can read.

(Antony and Cleopatra Act 1, Sc. 2: 10–11)

In summer's burning book of shame
A shimmer I can read. . .
In winter's frozen book of death
A silence I can read. . .
In time's ticking book of terror
A future I could not find. . .
In the cloud's soft book of rain
A fog smothered my view. . .

Majid, 10 yrs.

Here are a few more lines that I have tried with children as a basis for their own poems:

O word of fear (*Love's Labour's Lost*)
A killing frost (*Henry VIII*)
This is a brave night to cool a courtesan. (*King Lear*)
But soft, methinks I scent the morning air. (*Hamlet*)
Peace! – how the moon sleeps. . . (*The Merchant of Venice*)
Swift, swift, you dragons of the night. (*Cymbeline*)
The ox hath therefore stretched his yoke in vain. (A
   Midsummer Night's Dream)
I know a bank where the wild time blows,
Where oxlips and the nodding violet grows. . . (A
   Midsummer Night's Dream)

The teacher-poet Fred Sedgwick has written an excellent book about paying homage to Shakespeare through writing poems based on lines from the plays. The book contains many teaching ideas and examples of children's poems (*Shakespeare and the Young Writer*, Routledge, 1999). Anyone interested in children's creative writing will find the book both inspiring and practical.

One simple activity that helps children to enter memorably into Shakespeare's language is to imitate some of his lines. Use them as creative springboards, to unleash new possibilities. The teacher has to read carefully, looking for possible patterns, where a line or image might lend itself to innovation. For instance, early in *Hamlet* we find:

The air bites shrewdly.

This would be a simple enough pattern to innovate upon:

The sun dreams lazily.
The Moon snarls angrily.
The trees stand bitterly.
The stones wait patiently.

Macbeth has always been a good play to experience with Year 6. Whilst it seems obvious to write spells or charms arising from the witch's famous scene, there are other possibilities. For instance, children may be interested to hear that the expression 'he looked daggers at me' comes from Shakespeare. Hamlet states: 'I will speak daggers to her, but use none'. In *Macbeth*, the dagger is a central image both as a real object of murder and as a metaphor for 'there's daggers in men's smiles' (2.3.147). Macbeth wonders 'Art thou but a dagger of the mind'?

Ask the children what else might be seen in a smile, eyes, hands, tears, sobs, cries, pain, hearts? A year 6 group quickly gave me: 'There's hooks in men's eyes, there's sharks in men's promises, there's knives in men's hearts, there's a thief in men's promises'.

THERE'S DAGGERS IN MEN'S SMILES

There are icicles in a teacher's stare.
There's a forest in a bear's glare.

There's a Moon in a wolf's howl.
There's a question in a monk's cowl.

There are hooks in a crook's eyes,
There are sharks in a fox's lies,

There are knives in an ogre's wave,
There are thieves in the tyrant's grave.

There are tulips in women's lips.
There's a bee's sting in the ringmaster's whip.

Here are a few more lines plus mini examples of children's writing:

Celia:	Here come Monsieur Le Beau
Rosalind:	With his mouth full of news.
Rosalind:	Look, here comes the Duke
Celia:	With his eyes full of anger.

Look, here comes the storm,
With his eyes full of rage.

Here comes the snow,
With her heart full of peace.

Here comes the wind,
With his soul full of fear.

Here comes the rain,
With his mind full of trouble.

Libby, 9 yrs

**IN NATURE'S INFINITE BOOK OF SECRECY,
A LITTLE I CAN READ....**

In silence's book of secrets,
A little I can read...

In time's book of energy,
A little I can read...

Jacob, 9 yrs

HE WEARS THE ROSE OF YOUTH UPON HIM

He wears the violet flower of light upon him.
She wears the scarab of souls.
He wears the flower of love.
She wears the diamond of poison.
He wears the tree of trouble above his heart.
She holds the cracked heart of crumbling love near her heart.

Kieran, 9 yrs

O WORD OF FEAR

O world of power
O world of joy
O sword of glass
O rays of sorrow

Declan, 9 yrs

In this last example, Ellen takes different Shakespearean lines and puts them all together:

Look here comes the Cyclops,
With his eyes full of anger.

His invisible book of rage,
The little he can read . . .

He wears the belt of fear,
O thought of death,
A dying dream.

Look, here comes the dragon of gold,
With his wings packed with hate.

His unforgettable book of putrid horror,
The little he can read . . .

He wears the poppy of death,
O moment of memory,
A nightmare of tar.

Here comes the pixie of love,
With her heart full of gold.

Her hopeful book of forgiveness,
The little she can read . . .

She wears the ring of destiny,
O dream of power,

A replaced wrong.

Ellen, 9 yrs

Other possible Shakespearian lines that you might want to use:

I am as hot as molten lead, and as heavy too.

The stars will kiss the valleys first

Out of this nettle, danger, we pluck this flower, safety . . .

Uneasy lies the head that wears a crown

This is a brave night to cool a courtesan

But soft! methinks I scent the morning air

Peace! How the moon sleeps

Swift, swift, you dragons of the night

'Tis thought the King is dead; we will not stay.
The bay trees in our country are all withered.
And meteors fright the fixed stars of heaven,
The pale-faced moon looks bloody on the earth,
And lean-looked prophets whisper fearful change;
Rich men look sad, and ruffians dance and leap. . .

I'll give my jewels for a set of beads;
My gorgeous palace for a hermitage;
My figured goblets for a dish of wood;
My sceptre for a palmer's walking staff;
My subjects for a pair of carvèd saints;
And my large kingdom for a little grave;
A little, little grave, an obscure grave.

THE RIVER

I invented this pattern because I was working with a class of
year 5 children who had considerable experience in writing
poetry. I had worked with some of the children previously on
a 'gifted and talented' project. The teacher wanted me to
work on poems linked to her topic of rivers. I set the children
the challenge of creating a series of invented rivers. The rules
for writing were as follows:

1. Each verse has 3 lines.
2. Begin with the words 'The river of'.
3. Then write a noun, e.g. night, stars, dreams, confusion,
   hope, disasters, etc.
4. End the opening line with a verb that shows how the river
   moves, e.g. drifts, nudges, flows, cascades. . .
5. Line 2 begins with a preposition, e.g. by, beside, around,
   towards, past.
6. Then include a place, e.g. castle, town, city, tower.

7. Add on 'of' plus a noun, e.g. silence, wishes, scars.
8. The third line is a simile, starting with 'like'.

I've included this here to show the sorts of demands that can be placed upon more experienced writers that would not work with those who have been taught little about writing. There are writing challenges that would not be appropriate to ask of the less experienced struggler.

THE RIVER

The river of dreams drifts
Towards a castle of confusion
Like a comet's tail.

The river of night nudges
Past the city of silence
Like a velvet ribbon.

The river of imagination inches
Towards the cathedral of calm
Like a rainbow's curve.

The river of snowflakes slinks
By the forest of fear
Like a terrified trail.

The river of tigers' eyes twists
Round the hills of hatred
Like a witch's beckoning finger.

The river of frost flows
By the market of mirth
Like a cobra's body swaying.

The river of disasters dives
Beneath the land of lanterns
Like a thread torn from Cinderella's gown.

CHAPTER 8
Poetry slams

Some schools hold an annual poetry slam. Children can perform in groups or individually. Time will need to be given to practising and the children should think about the fundamentals of performance:

- Speak your poem clearly.
- Make sure the volume is loud enough to be heard.
- Use expression and rhythm.
- Vary volume, pace and expression for effect.
- Use dramatic pauses.
- Use simple movement or percussion.

To judge the slam you will need a panel of judges who mark out of a hundred, each focusing on one of the following elements:

- The performance
- The quality of the poem (if written by the performers)
- The volume of the audience's response.

Performance poems, rapid rhymes and rapping lend themselves to slams.

BUY THIS POEM

This poem's up for sale,
It's ready in the frame.
It's got all the things
A poem should contain.

It's got a handsome hero
Saving those in danger,
A love interest resulting in
A baby in a manger.

It's got rhythm, rhyme and skills
And a pack of wolves that kills,
Liquid supersonic metre,
Duplicating by the litre.

The comic duo are your mates,
The criminals you love to hate.
The narrator, who's quite a bore,
The interval, the half time-score.

This poem is for sale,
'Come on' -
This poem is so loveable,
        Incredible,
            Spreadible,
                Edible.

In fact, forget it.
Just put away your money, funny honey.
'Cos I don't want your wealth,
            your health,
                to be left on the shelf.
This poem goes to one who deserves it.
And that is 'myself'.

Teddy Corbett, 15 yrs

To help children develop a sense of rhythm and rhyme play, a few musical warm-ups:

- Clap the beat of names and other words.
- Pass a beat around the group.
- Then change the beat and pass it on.
- Pass rhymes round a circle. These words work well: *plain, toast, meat, slap, mash, bat, pay, rest, pill, fit, fine, sing, think, slip, got, hop, bump, feel, phone, might, tries, hope, weed, pail, stoat, dream, place, alive, coal, fake, book, tar, dock, black, spout, good, bed, mad, boy, pay, late, three, cry, grow, blue, name, grave, mine, soon, rule, joke, bug.*

Use a local map or atlas to list place names that have rhymes. Use these to make a simple rhyming poem to perform:

In Crewe
I felt blue.

In Gloucester
I lost her.

CHAPTER 9
Using the images

Pages 168–9 provides images to photocopy and use for writing. Interactive whiteboards mean that using photos, artwork, music and video clips has become a daily part of children's educational experiences. I am always armed with a memory stick that has on it images of art such as Dali and Magritte, as well as photos of animals, insects, people, places and video clips ready to use for writing stimuli. I have a very simple process for using these images, as follows.

THE PROCESS

Get the children to look at the image of the frog and make a list down the centre of their page of the key things that they can see. For instance, if you look at the photo of the frog, you could write down:

Eyes

Legs

Toes

Skin

Now take each idea in turn and use a little bit of technique (alliteration or imagery) to begin to develop each idea:

The frog's black eyes bulge like berries.

Its mottled leg curves.

Toes splayed out.

The frog's skin is like a stained map.

You can also imagine what you might hear or what might happen:

It sits, gulping air,

Staring at you,

With tight lips.

The penguin image can be tackled in the same way. I would start with a simple list:

Beak

Eyes

Wings

Feet

Also remind the children how penguins move – they waddle along.

It is also worth collecting postcards of paintings whenever you visit an art gallery. These can make excellent starting points for writing poems. The fact that each child has their own image and can hold it somehow adds to the impact.

Each child has a different picture to write about and therefore a chance to approach the writing individually. You can show them how to tackle writing about an image by using a picture on the whiteboard and composing a poem on a flip chart. Show the children how they should look carefully at their chosen picture and list words, phrases, ideas, memories . . . based on what they can see. These can then be built up into a poem.

One simple way into writing is to start with the line 'In this painting I can see . . .'. Then make a list of 5 or 6 things that can be seen – let's say a bridge, the moon, stars, a river, some trees. Place these in the centre of the page and begin to build either side of each word, e.g.

In this picture I can see –
A melancholy **moon** glowing
Bright **stars** like tin tacks
The silver **river** sliding by
The **bridge** hunched like an old man
Thin **trees** whispering.

In a year 4 class in Abbeymeads Primary School in Swindon, we created a shared poem about a wintry scene:

The frosty fog grips the forest in its clenched fist.
Fluffy branches sway.
A slim branch leans out like a slash of lightning.
The icy trees prickle.
In the distance the mountains frown furiously.
A powerful wind scratches at your skin.
The dusty snow drifts like a seagull's feather.

Mr Smith's class + Pie Corbett

This poem was written by Nico who was in my village school in Kent. An interesting writer – he took his time and chose words with care. I remember him saying to me once, 'What I like about writing is that you never know what is going to happen'. I agree. He was writing about a self-portrait by Stanley Spencer:

THE COAL MINER

His blackened out face matches the pitch black wall.
His rigid chin is like the humps that a camel would have.
His long neck juts up with strength and authority.
His old torn sweater is smothered in dust and smudged by
    splinters of coal.
His stern face glares at the dark passage to nowhere.

Nico, 8 years

Finally, this poem by Claire is a good example of writing that is almost a descriptive paragraph. When planning literacy, it is worth teaching poetry before narrative as many of the writing strategies will be useful when composing stories.

THE POKER ROOM
(after a painting by Edward Burra)

The knife lies motionless in the murky room.
The hand quivers, a sudden crash,
A streak of lightning stuns the silent sky.
A breeze blown, the cigarette smoke streaks
In a misty haze out through the door.
The table shudders as the stranger reaches
For the dusty gin bottle.
The carved ring presents –
An omen.
A crumpled week old paper
Floats to the ground.
Blurred dots of the dice roll
To show a six.
The stranger cackles,
Startling.

Claire, 10 yrs

CHAPTER 10

Ideas for publishing and performances

Children's poetry should be published on a regular basis with the minimum of fuss. Publishing should be the natural outcome of most poetry sessions.

1. Each child has their own beautiful homemade book and their poems are glued in. This should be added to over the year.
2. Class anthologies are produced each term or at least yearly.
3. Poems are turned into posters or made into book markers.
4. Lines or phrases from poems are used as screen savers.
5. Poems are performed to other classes and in assemblies as a regular aspect of school life.
6. Poems are recorded on to CD or DVD and these are sold to parents and the community.
7. Poetry shows are put on whenever an author visits a school – the author performs or reads and so do children.
8. Poems are sent to local newspapers, radio and TV stations and entered into competitions.
9. Poems are put on the school website.
10. Poems are sent to a poet whose work has inspired the class.
11. Poems are displayed imaginatively, e.g. in boxes, as origami doors or windows with flaps, on haiku posters, as scrolls, in envelopes, on a school poetry trail. . .
12. Poems are spoken over images, photos or short films and turned into PowerPoint or other formatted multimedia presentations.

13. Poems are performed with music and action.
14. A special 'school poetry book' is kept and the very best poems from any class are written into the book.

Appendices

DVDS, CDS AND WEBSITES

Let's Write Poetry – four BBC programmes on DVD, featuring Kit Wright, Brian Patten, Val Bloom and Michael Rosen plus many other poems read aloud. They advertise it as 'poetry writing for years 5 and 6' but you could use parts of it with anyone from year 2 to year 8. Order from 0870 830 8000 or online from www.bbcactive.com/ schoolshop

Poems Out Loud – selected by Brian Moses, published by Hodder Children's Books – a CD and Book. About to be reissued as *Walking my Iguana*. This has the best recording of 'The Tyger', read by John Agard.

The Essential Dylan Thomas – Naxos Audio Books – the beginning of 'Under Milk Wood' read by Richard Burton will not fail to grip the children. Write imitative descriptions of dawn.

The Spoken Word – historic recordings from the British Library – includes Alfred Noyes reading 'The Highwayman' as well as Robert Frost, Walter de la Mare, William Carlos Williams – available from the British Library.

Poetry Archives – www.poetryarchive.org. Listen to poets reading – plus some lesson plans and ideas. Also buy CDs for classroom use. Excellent resource – poets include Valerie Bloom, Michael Rosen, Wes Magee, Judith Nicholls, Allan Ahlberg, Brian Moses, James Berry, Charles Causley, Simon Armitage, Kit Wright, Vernon Scannell, Adrian Mitchell, Edwin Morgan. Also good links to other sites.

Poetry Class – www.poetryclass.net. This is the online poetry classroom. Plenty of great ideas.

Poetryzone – www.poetryzone.co.uk. The best poetry site for children and teachers in the country if not the world. There are lesson ideas, book reviews, children's own poems and poets talking about their writing. It is lively, fun and provides all the 'umph' that you need.

Poetry Book Society – www.poetrybooks.co.uk. Worth joining because it keeps a steady stream of quality poetry books coming into the school – or your personal collection.

The British Haiku Society – www.haikusoc.ndu.co.uk. Order 'The Haiku Kit' from here, an invaluable photocopiable resource for teaching. Only £4.

Waning Moon Press – www.haiku.insouthsea.co.uk. Complete with haiku teaching notes for primary or secondary. Excellent resource.

ANTHOLOGIES

The Works: Poems for Key Stage 2 – Poems referred to in this book can be found in this volume or in **The Works: Poems for Key Stage 1** – both edited by Pie Corbett, published by Macmillan Children's Books. The key stage 2 book would be ideal also for years 7 and 8.

The King's Pyjamas – edited by Pie Corbett – Belitha Press. A jolly collection for year 3/key stage 1. Also *Footprints in the Butter* – ed. Pie Corbett and published by Belitha. A collection of riddles.

Masala – edited by Debjani Chatterjee – poems from India, Bangladesh, Pakistan and Sri Lanka – published by Macmillan Children's Books. A great collection – a must for every school.

One River, Many Creeks – poems from all around the world – edited by Valerie Bloom – published by Macmillan Children's Books. Also **Around the World in Eighty Poems**, edited by James Berry – both books contain good poems from other places and cultures.

Talking Drums – edited by Veronique Tadjo – published by A & C Black – a good collection of poems from Africa, south of the Sahara.

The Works 4 – Pie Corbett and Gaby Morgan – a fat collection of hundreds of poems about all sorts of subjects that are not normally on the curriculum. Macmillan Children's Books provides the best selection of anthologies.

Black's Rhyming and Spelling Dictionary – published by A & C Black – the best rhyming dictionary – ideal for rhyming games.

Individual collections
Collected Poems for Children – Ted Hughes – Faber and Faber.

Going to the Fair – Charles Causley – Macmillan Children's Books.

Great Snakes – Kit Wright – Viking – look out for his forthcoming collected poems for children from Macmillan.

The Oldest Girl in the World – Carol Anne Duffy – Faber.

Manifold Manor – Philip Gross – Faber.

The Snollygoster – Helen Dunmore – Scholastic.

Juggling with Gerbils – Brian Patten – Penguin.

Taking out the Tigers – Brian Moses — Macmillan.

Also any books of poems by James Berry, Valerie Bloom, Wes Magee, James Carter, Jan Dean, Roger Stevens, John Foster, Paul Cookson, Andrew Fusek Peters, Jackie Kay, John Mole, John Rice, Judith Nicholls, Vernon Scannell, Gareth Owen, Simon Armitage, Carol Ann Duffy, George Mackay Brown, Edwin Morgan, Gillian Clarke, Sue Cowling, Ian McMillan, Miroslav Holub, Matthew Sweeney.

10 books to read about teaching poetry writing that will last you a lifetime:

1. **The Way to Write** – John Fairfax and John Moat, Elm Tree Books. This book looks at how words work. It will provide you with in-depth understanding.

2. **Poetry in the Making** – Ted Hughes – Faber and Faber – this will help you not only to understand poetry but also to establish key principles about writing. Essential read for all teachers of English.

3. **Caterpaults and Kingfishers** – Pie Corbett and Brian Moses – OUP – some people still say it's the best book they have ever read on writing. Lots of models and ideas.

4. **Read My Mind** – Fred Sedgwick – Routledge – young children, poetry and learning – in-depth read with many practical ideas and examples.

5. **Wishes Lies and Dreams** – Kenneth Koch – Vintage Books – quirky stuff – ideas and examples for helping children play with language.

6. **Rose, Where did You Get that Red** – Kenneth Koch – published by Vintage Books – ideas for teaching classic poetry to children through responding by writing.

7. **Creating Writers** – James Carter – Routledge – a fantastic creative writing manual, packed with ideas and based on discussions with writers.

8. **Page to Stage** – James Carter – David Fulton Publishers – poetry and performance – complete with a CD. Lots of models and ideas. Also try *Just Imagine*.

9. **The Poetry Book for Primary Schools** – edited by Anthony Wilson with Sian Hughes – ideas, essays and examples of writing.

10. **Shakespeare and the Young Writer** – by Fred Sedgwick – Routledge – wonderful in-depth exploration of children responding to Shakespeare through writing.

You can read poetry books and magazines and research at the Poetry Library (0207 921 0943). Their website also has an education section.

HOW TO BOOK A POET IN SCHOOL

I have not said anything about having a poet in school – but in my view every child should meet a writer at least once a year – poet, author or storyteller. They should also have a theatrical experience annually as well as the chance to work with an artist of some sort. The book *Our Thoughts are Bees: Writers Working in Schools* by Mandy Coe and Jean Sprackland (Wordplay Press) provides details about working with poets in school as well as providing useful listings. If you really are unsure who to ask or what to do, write to Speaking of Books, 105 John Humphries House, 4 Stockwell Street, Greenwich, London SE10 9JN. A teacher-friendly agency that will help arrange school visits, order books for the visit, etc.

Bibliography

Brautigan, R. (1965) 'Period Piece', in *Wild Dog* (18), 17 July 1965: 19.

Collins, B. (2007) *The Trouble with Poetry: And Other Poems.* Random House.

Corbett, P. (Ed.) (2006) *The Works: Poems for Key Stage 2.* London: Macmillan Children's Books.

Corbett, P. and Moses, B. (2002) *The Works: Poems on every subject and or every ocassion.* London: Macmillan Children's Books.

McMillan, I. (1998) *I Found this Shirt: Poems and Prose from the Centre.* Carcanet.

Shonagon, Shei (2006) *The Pillow Book.* Penguin Classics.

Simic, C. (2007) *Dimestore Alchemy: The Art of Joseph Connell (New York Book Review Classics).* New York: Review of Books Inc.

Steven, Wallace (2001) *Harmonium (Faber Poetry).* Faber and Faber.

Strickland, Stephanie (2005) 'Here Comes Everybody': http://herecomeseverybody.blogspot.com/2005/03/stephanie-strickland-is-print-and-new.html

Tzara, Tristan (1918) 'Dada Manifesto' and 'Lecture on Dada' (1922). Translated from French by R. Motherwell in Motherwell, R. (1989) *The Dada Painters and Poets: An Anthology.* Harvard University Press.

Williams, William Carlos (1954) *Selected Essays of William Carlos Williams.* Random House.

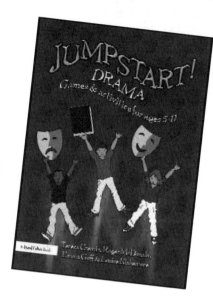